World War II:
The War in the Pacific

by Don Nardo

America's WARS

Lucent Books, P.O. Box 289011, San Diego, CA 92198-9011

Books in the America's Wars Series:

The Revolutionary War
The Indian Wars
The War of 1812
The Mexican-American War
The Civil War
The Spanish-American War

World War I
World War II: The War in the Pacific
World War II: The War in Europe
The Korean War
The Vietnam War
The Persian Gulf War

Library of Congress Cataloging-in-Publication Data

Nardo, Don, 1947-
  World War II : the war in the Pacific / by Don Nardo.
      p.   cm. — (America's wars series)
  Includes bibliographical references and index.
  Summary: Examines the action in the Pacific theater of World War
II, focusing on the confrontation between the United States and
Japan.
  ISBN 1-56006-408-0
  1. World War, 1939-1945—Campaigns—Pacific Area—Juvenile
literature.   2. World War, 1939-1945—Japan—Juvenile literature.
3. World War, 1939-1945—United States—Juvenile literature.
4. Japan—History—1926-1945—Juvenile literature.   5. United
States—History—1933-1945—Juvenile literature.   6. Pacific Area—
History—Juvenile literature.   [1. World War, 1939-1945—
Campaigns—Pacific Area. 2. Japan—History—1926-1945.   3. United
States—History—1933-1945.] I. Title.   II. Series.
D767.N36   1991
940.54'26—dc20
                                                              91-16727

Contents

Foreword 4

Chronology of Events 6

Introduction: A Fanatic Belief in the Glory of War 7

Chapter 1: Sons of the Rising Sun—The Long Road to War 9

Chapter 2: "Climb Mount Niitaka"—The Attack on Pearl Harbor 21

Chapter 3: From Batavia to Bataan—The Japanese Empire Expands 32

Chapter 4: Turning Point at Midway—The United States Strikes Back 42

Chapter 5: "In Death There Is Life"—Japan's Desperate Defense 58

Chapter 6: Nuclear Dawn—The United States Drops the Atom Bomb 73

Chapter 7: "A Better World Shall Emerge"—Surrender and Aftermath 83

Glossary 91

For Further Reading 92

Works Consulted 93

Index 94

Photo Credits 96

About the Author 96

Foreword

War, justifiable or not, is a descent into madness. George Washington, America's first president and commander-in-chief of its armed forces, wrote that his most fervent wish was "to see this plague of mankind, war, banished from the earth." Most, if not all of the forty presidents who succeeded Washington have echoed similar sentiments. Despite this, not one generation of Americans since the founding of the republic has been spared the maelstrom of war. In its brief history of just over two hundred years, the United States has been a combatant in eleven major wars. And four of those conflicts have occurred in the last fifty years.

America's reasons for going to war have differed little from those of most nations. Political, social, and economic forces were at work which either singly or in combination ushered America into each of its wars. A desire for independence motivated the Revolutionary War. The fear of annihilation led to the War of 1812. A related fear, that of having the nation divided, precipitated the Civil War. The need to contain an aggressor nation brought the United States into the Korean War. And territorial ambition lay behind the Mexican-American and the Indian Wars. Like all countries, America, at different times in its history, has been victimized by these forces and its citizens have been called to arms.

Whatever reasons may have been given to justify the use of military force, not all of America's wars have been popular. From the Revolutionary War to the Vietnam War, support of the people has alternately waxed and waned. For example, less than half of the colonists backed America's war of independence. In fact, most historians agree that at least one-third were committed to maintaining America's colonial status. During the Spanish-American War, a strong antiwar movement also developed. Resistance to the war was so high that the Democratic party made condemning the war a significant part of its platform in an attempt to lure voters into voting Democratic. The platform stated that "the burning issue of imperialism growing out of the Spanish war involves the very existence of the Republic and the destruction of our free institutions." More recently, the Vietnam War divided the nation like no other conflict had since the Civil War. The mushrooming antiwar movements in most major cities and colleges throughout the United States did more to bring that war to a conclusion than did actions on the battlefield.

Yet, there have been wars which have enjoyed overwhelming public support. World Wars I and II were popular because people believed that the survival of America's democratic institutions was at stake. In both wars, the American people rallied with an enthusiasm and spirit of self-sacrifice that was remarkable for a country with such a diverse population. Support for food and fuel rationing, the purchase of war bonds, a high rate of voluntary enlistments, and countless other forms of voluntarism, were characteristic of the people's response to those wars. Most recently, the Persian Gulf War prompted an unprecedented show of support even though the United States was not directly threatened by the conflict. Rallies in support of U.S. troops were widespread. Tens of thousands of individuals, including families, friends, and well-wishers of the troops sent packages of food, cosmetics, clothes, cassettes, and suntan oil. And even more supporters wrote letters to unknown soldiers that were forwarded to the military front. In fact, most public opinion polls revealed that up to 90 percent of all Americans approved of their nation's involvement.

The complex interplay of events and purposes that leads to military conflict should be included in a history of any war. A simple chronicling of battles and casualty lists at best offers only a partial history of war. Wars do not spontaneously erupt; nor does their memory perish. They are driven by underlying causes, fueled by policymakers, fought and supported by citizens, and remembered by those plotting a nation's future. For these reasons wars, or the fear of wars, will always leave an indelible stamp on any nation's history and influence its future.

The purpose of this series is to provide a full understanding of America's Wars by presenting each war in a historical context. Each of the twelve volumes focuses on the events that led up to the war, the war itself, its impact on the home front, and its aftermath and influence upon future conflicts. The unique personalities, the dramatic acts of courage and compassion, as well as the despair and horror of war are all presented in this series. Together, they show why America's wars have dominated American consciousness in the past as well as how they guide many political decisions of today. In these vivid and objective accounts, students will gain an understanding of why America became involved in these conflicts, and how historians, military and government officials, and others have come to understand and interpret that involvement.

Chronology of Events

1192
Yoritomo becomes the first shogun, establishing a military order in Japan.

1637
Japan expels all foreigners from the country.

1854
Commodore Perry from the United States intimidates the Japanese into signing a treaty that allows Americans to enter Japanese ports.

1868
Japan abandons feudalism and begins building a modern state.

1904–1905
Japan fights and defeats Russia in Russo-Japanese War.

1914–1918
World War I.

1929
U.S. stock market crashes; beginning of worldwide depression that also affects Japan.

1931
Japan invades Manchuria in China.

1936
Japan allies itself with Nazi Germany and Italy.

1939
August 2 Albert Einstein writes to President Roosevelt proposing the building of an atomic bomb.
September 21 Germany invades Poland. World War II begins in Europe.

1941
December 7 Japanese attack Pearl Harbor and other locations in Asia and the Pacific. The Pacific War begins.
December 22 Japan invades the Philippines.

1942
April 18 James Doolitle leads American bombing raid on Tokyo.

June 4 United States defeats Japan in Battle of Midway.

August 7 U.S. Marines land on Guadalcanal.

1943
February 8 Japanese evacuate Guadalcanal.

November 1 U.S. troops assault the Solomon Islands.

1944
June 19 United States decisively defeats Japan in Battle of the Philippine Sea.

October 21 Americans under General MacArthur return to the Philippines.

October 23–25 United States wins greatest sea battle in history at Leyte Gulf, Philippines.

1945
February 19 U.S. Marines storm Iwo Jima, a gateway to Japan.

March 9 American bombers create fire storm that destroys most of Tokyo.

April 1 U.S. troops attack Okinawa.

April 12 President Roosevelt dies. Harry Truman becomes president.

July 16 First atomic bomb tested in New Mexico desert.

August 6 United States drops atomic bomb on Hiroshima.

August 8 Soviet Union declares war on Japan.

August 9 United States drops atomic bomb on Nagasaki.

September 2 Japan surrenders to Allies. Pacific War ends.

October 24 United Nations is officially established.

1948
Tojo and other Japanese war criminals executed.

A Fanatic Belief in the Glory of War

On December 7, 1941, Japan suddenly and decisively attacked the U.S. naval base at Pearl Harbor in Hawaii. The huge and powerful Japanese forces then swept across eastern Asia and the islands of the Pacific Ocean. Within three days, dozens of nations and nearly four-fifths of the people on earth were involved in a massive global conflict.

Almost none of the nations involved had wanted war. Most Westerners—the Americans, Canadians, British, and others—had done everything they could to avoid becoming entangled in the hostilities. They looked upon war as a destructive last resort for settling their differences with Japan and other nations.

By contrast, the Japanese did want war with the West. Their view of war was very different. The Japanese were fanatic in their belief that war was necessary, useful, and glorious. Most Japanese thought that it was better to die fighting than to live with dishonor.

Fighting the "Barbarians"

These warlike attitudes stemmed partly from Japanese religious beliefs, which stressed that the gods favored the Japanese above all other peoples. Foreigners were inferior "barbarians." There-fore, it was only natural and fitting that the Japanese conquer or destroy those who threatened them.

Japanese attitudes about war were also influenced by their cul-ture. Since ancient times, the Japanese had glorified war. Warriors and military leaders were respected above all others. According to the warrior's code, to die in battle was the greatest possible honor.

For the Japanese, war with the West was also a matter of self-defense. Japanese leaders saw the conflict as absolutely necessary to the survival of their country. They were convinced that the Western nations wanted to keep the Japanese weak and submissive while exploiting Japan's economic markets. The ultimate goal of the United States, the Japanese believed, was to "westernize" Japan and thereby destroy Japanese culture. According to this view, Japan must sooner or later clash with and destroy the United States and other Western nations that threatened its existence.

The Japanese leaders passed these ideas to their people through a constant and effective campaign of propaganda. The government controlled what was reported in the press and decided what would be taught in the schools. Japanese children learned that Americans and other Westerners were corrupt and weak and could be defeated easily by the Japanese.

The Americans and other Westerners found the Japanese attitudes about war strange. Never before had U.S. soldiers faced an enemy so fanatic about war and so willing to die for honor. This was one of the reasons that the Americans were surprised by the attack on Pearl Harbor. They were unprepared for an adversary so willing to go to war, so ready to risk the fate of an entire nation in a bloody global conflict.

And so, the Pacific War was not only a military struggle but also a clash of attitudes. For the United States, the conflict was a grim, unfortunate, but necessary task. For Japan, it was a glorious means to achieving an even more glorious destiny.

Japan's attack on Pearl Harbor weakened American naval power. Enemy torpedoes damaged the USS Maryland (left), capsized the USS Oklahoma (right), and caused hundreds of American deaths.

CHAPTER ONE

Sons of the Rising Sun—The Long Road to War

n the late 1930s, on the eve of World War II, the United States and Japan were two powerful nations uneasily facing each other across the wide Pacific Ocean. The United States, resting at the center of the North American continent, bordered the eastern side of the Pacific. U.S. influence extended to many countries in the Pacific area, largely because of ownership of the Hawaiian Islands, located about two thousand miles off the coast of California.

Bordering the Western edge of the Pacific, at a distance of some five thousand miles from the United States, was the island nation of Japan. Located off the coast of the continent of Asia, Japan was a relatively small country. The combined total of its more than three thousand islands is an area slightly smaller than the state of California, barely one-twelfth the size of the United States.

The ocean was not the only barrier that separated the United States and Japan. Attitudes about politics and international relations were almost completely opposite in the two countries. The United States was one of the world's leading democracies, controlled by an elected president and Congress. In the 1930s, the country was largely isolationist, desiring to stay out of foreign disputes and wars.

By contrast, Japan was a dictatorship, ruled by a few powerful military leaders. The Japanese militarists were expansionists, seeking to extend their influence and control over other lands by any means necessary, including war. In fact, the Japanese leaders saw war with the United States and other "inferior" foreigners as essential to the continued survival and expansion of the Japanese people.

The Divinity of the Emperor

Historic evidence suggests that for as many as two thousand years, a succession of emperors has ruled Japan. For many centuries, these rulers governed the land, made political policy, enforced laws, and waged war. In time, however, as powerful warlords transformed Japan into a feudal society, the role of the emperors became more ceremonial. Eventually, people regarded the emperor as a spiritual leader who stayed in the background and became involved in affairs of state only when absolutely necessary.

The shoguns and other Japanese leaders learned to take advantage of the spiritual image of the emperor. They pictured him as semidivine, having descended directly from the sun-goddess Amaterasu. Invoking the name of an emperor became an effective way to unify and control the people. For instance, the shogun often convinced his emperor to endorse unpopular laws. People then tended to accept these laws as the will of the gods. Leaders also used the image of the emperor to instill feelings of pride and patriotism. The Japanese emperors were considered the only living gods in the world, and this made the Japanese people feel that they were special, favored by heaven above all other races.

This national worship of the emperor persisted into modern times. In 1890, the government declared in writing that "the Emperor is sacred and inviolable [untouchable]." Elaborate rituals surrounded him. No one could look directly at the emperor when he passed by, and

Hirohito was the emperor of Japan during and after World War II.

his personal name could never be spoken aloud. People swore complete allegiance to him, some even risking their lives to carry his picture out of burning buildings. To the pre–World War II Japanese, the emperor was a symbol of the country's honor and also a direct link between the people and the gods.

In ancient times, the Japanese revered the samurai for their loyalty, discipline, and ferocity. During World War II, Japanese pilots (above) and Japanese soldiers continued the fighting tradition of the samurai.

A Society of Warriors

Japan's traditions of militarism and hatred of foreigners, which ultimately plunged the world into war, originated centuries before. For nearly two thousand years, the Japanese recognized the absolute authority of a succession of emperors. Each one, the Japanese believed, was divine, descended directly from the sun-goddess Amaterasu. Confident that the goddess favored them above other peoples, the Japanese looked upon foreigners as inferior. To honor Amaterasu, Japanese leaders adopted the image of the sun as their special symbol and referred to their nation as the "land of the rising sun." They chose to remain isolated from foreign, "barbaric" nations and had little contact with the outside world.

The Samurai—Proud Warriors

The samurai emerged as a distinct social class in Japan in the eleventh century. They were skillful, fearless warriors who trained for years to master the use of razor-sharp samurai swords and other forms of self-defense. Groups of samurai warriors were loyal to various powerful warlords and to the shoguns, who were themselves samurai. The samurai became the most feared, respected, and honored group in Japanese society.

Even after the rule of the shoguns ended in 1868, samurai influences remained. Among these was a strong sense of honor and a strict code of behavior that emphasized loyalty to authority, courage, and the choice of suicide over surrender. Most Japanese soldiers in World War II followed the samurai code of conduct enthusiastically.

The samurai warrior of the 1650s wore several pads of protective iron armor. He carried two swords, gripping the longer one with both hands.

Extreme militaristic attitudes took firm root in Japan beginning in the year 1192. A powerful warlord named Yoritomo seized control of most of the country and established a formal military order in Japanese society. Yoritomo called himself the shogun (general). He became the supreme overlord of the Japanese empire.

In the new feudal order, individual warlords ruled sections of the country and maintained forces of loyal warriors. The shogun oversaw these warlords. He was the absolute ruler of the country and answered only to the emperor. Since the emperor was thought to be a living god, he usually did not involve himself in everyday affairs unless the shogun requested him to do so. The shogun allowed people to farm and fish in exchange for occasional military service. For his permanent military staff, the shogun employed full-time professional warriors known as samurai. It was this samurai military order that planted the seeds of Japanese fanaticism about war. The samurai glorified war, believing that it was the most effective means of solving problems. They maintained a strict social code that emphasized loyalty and honor above all other virtues. For instance, a samurai owed complete allegiance to his shogun and the emperor and pledged to lay down his life for them if necessary. There was an intense pride about one's name and honor. When accused of dishonor, many Japanese people committed hara-kiri, or *seppuku*, a gruesome ritual suicide in which a knife or sword is plunged in and up through the stomach.

The glorification of war and a fanatic loyalty to the person in power became a part of the character of the Japanese people.

The Outside World Closes In

Japanese militaristic and antiforeign attitudes further intensified after the country started to deal with the outside world. Under the leadership of the shoguns, Japanese society had remained largely unchanged and isolated from other nations until the 1800s. By that time, the United States and other Western nations recognized that trade with Japan could be very lucrative. By opening a trade relationship, the United States could establish a valuable trade route to China. Also, U.S. whalers who hunted in the waters near Japan could use Japanese ports to resupply their ships. In 1853, Commodore Matthew Perry sailed a large squadron of American warships to Japan and demanded that the Japanese sign a treaty with the United States. The Japanese indicated that they were not interested. But Perry hinted that if the Japanese did not agree to the terms of the treaty, the United States might use some kind of force. Intimidated by U.S. military might, the Japanese reluctantly signed the treaty in 1854, agreeing to allow American ships to resupply in Japanese ports. Seeing the opportunity to exploit

Hara-Kiri—Death with Honor

Literally translated as "belly-cutting," hara-kiri was the common method of suicide practiced by the samurai and others in feudal Japan. Most Japanese prefer the older term *seppuku* to describe the ritual. The proper procedure was to stab a sword or knife into the left side of the stomach, slash across to the right side, then slice into the chest and push downward, forming a cross on the front of the body. If the person was still conscious after this, the last step was to cut the throat.

Because hara-kiri was a slow, painful form of suicide, it was thought to be a way of showing self-control and courage. Often, samurai warriors committed hara-kiri after defeat in battle to avoid the dishonor of capture. Sometimes, a warrior performed the ritual after the death of his lord in order to show loyalty. The tradition of hara-kiri survived along with the samurai code of honor into modern times. This was due to the popularity of plays like the eighteenth-century drama *Chushingura*, or the Tale of the Loyal Retainers. These plays glorified the idea of ritual suicide and influenced millions of ordinary Japanese citizens. Thousands of Japanese soldiers in World War II chose this form of death rather than surrender.

Japanese markets, Great Britian and other nations immediately established trade relations with the Japanese, who now felt they had no choice but to cooperate.

The majority of Japanese were embarrassed and angry about the concessions made to the foreigners, believing that the outsiders would soon try to take over Japan. Japanese leaders decided that there was only one way their country could survive. It must become militarily and materially equal to Western countries like the United States.

The Incredible Transformation

In 1868, the Japanese began one of the most ambitious undertakings ever attempted by a nation. Their goal was to transform their backward country into a modern world power in the space of only a few years. As a first step, they abandoned feudalism and emphasized nationalism—loyalty to the nation instead of loyalty to individual warlords and shoguns. Loyalty to the emperor was also stressed, for the Japanese still looked upon him as a living god.

Although the rule of the shoguns had been eliminated, Japan was still run by a powerful military elite. In only two decades, they managed to completely restructure the country's political, military, and educational institutions, forcing all Japanese to work toward a single national aim. That aim was to make the country as strong as possible. For instance, schoolchildren were taught that the Japanese must be strong and aggressive in order to survive. In addition, the government built many factories that began to manufacture modern ships, guns, and other weapons. To help pay for these advances, the Japanese borrowed heavily from U.S. and other foreign banks. Eventually, Japan repaid many of these debts and maintained sizable investments in these banks.

Japan wanted to use its new weapons to expand its borders. This was a complete reversal of its former isolationism. Believing that the country needed fresh land and resources to make it more powerful, the new government became aggressive and tried to expand into neighboring countries. For hundreds of years, Japan had been an empire only in name. Now it would become an empire in fact.

The powerful, modernized Japanese army fought wars against China (1894–1895) and Russia (1904–1905) and won both conflicts. From the Chinese, Japan gained the island of Formosa (now Taiwan), south of Japan. From the Russians, the Japanese gained control of Korea, located only a few miles west of the Japanese home islands. After defeating Russia, the Japanese bragged openly that they had destroyed the myth of the supposed superiority of the white race.

Continued Japanese Aggression

After Japan's victories over China and Russia, the Western countries recognized that Japan was a threatening military power in the Far East. Whenever possible, Western countries tried to limit that power. For example, in 1922, shortly after the end of World War I, an international conference was held in Washington, D.C. to establish limits on weapons. One of the resolutions voted on by the Western powers put a limit on the number of warships Japan could build. This angered the Japanese, who believed that the United States and its allies wanted to keep Japan weak and submissive. Japan's extreme militarists used this incident and others to fuel warlike attitudes among the Japanese people. They sought to carry on the ancient samurai warrior traditions and strike back at any and all who opposed them. One Japanese official threatened, "Japan must no longer let the impudence of the white man go unpunished."

Making good on this threat, the Japanese began a series of warlike maneuvers. The first was the sudden and brutal invasion of the Chinese province of Manchuria in 1931. The Japanese felt that the invasion was justified, partly because it would help ensure the continued survival and prosperity of Japan. Between 1868 and 1930, Japan's population had risen from thirty million to more than sixty-five million, and the country badly needed coal, oil, farmland, and other resources that Manchuria possessed in abundance. The Japanese militarists also justified the invasion on the grounds that the Japanese had a right to exploit "inferior" peoples. One member of the government claimed, "From the fact of divine descent of the Japanese people proceeds their immeasurable superiority to the natives of other countries in courage and intelligence."

There was little opposition to Japan's aggression. The Chinese were too weak militarily to fight and appealed to the Western powers for help. Because they were preoccupied with the problems of the Great Depression, which had begun in 1929, the United States, Great Britain, and other countries hardly reacted to the takeover of Manchuria. They verbally condemned the action but allowed Japan to keep its prize. This emboldened the Japanese, and in 1932 they made Manchuria into a Japanese-governed state, changing its name to Manchukuo. They also continued to build up their armed forces, producing thousands of warplanes and hundreds of modern ships, in direct violation of the 1922 shipbuilding ban.

In 1936 and 1937, Japan made three more hostile moves. In each instance, the United States and other Western powers failed to act decisively against the growing Japanese threat. First, the Japanese signed an agreement of mutual cooperation, called the Anti-Comintern Pact, with the German Nazis led by Adolf Hitler.

Second, Japan invaded the heartland of China, intending to gain control of more valuable natural resources and farmland. Third, Japan joined Germany and Italy, two other militaristic states, to form the Axis powers. Each vowed to support the others if they were attacked. Because the three countries showed hostile intentions and were heavily arming themselves, most other nations saw the Axis alliance as a disturbing threat to world peace.

A Change of American Attitudes

The main reason that the United States did not act to stop Japan's numerous acts of aggression was that the Americans wanted to stay out of foreign disputes whenever possible. The United States had not always had this attitude. In the 1800s, the United States often sought to expand its influence and holdings in other parts of the world. But by the early 1900s, many Americans expressed less and less enthusiasm for the country getting involved in affairs in little-known, faraway lands.

As a result, when World War I erupted in Europe in 1914, U.S. leaders were reluctant to commit the nation to fighting. Although the United States eventually did fight in the war, most

Japan signed an agreement of mutual cooperation with German leader Adolf Hitler (above). Japan also joined Germany and Italy in the Axis alliance.

Franklin D. Roosevelt

The thirty-second president of the United States, Franklin Delano Roosevelt (1882–1945) served three terms, a total of twelve years, longer than any other president. He was one of the most important and influential leaders of the twentieth century. Roosevelt came from a wealthy family and worked his way up through various political offices, including state senator, assistant secretary of the navy, and governor of the state of New York.

Although stricken with polio and confined to a wheelchair, Roosevelt courageously ran for president in 1932. He promised to get the country out of the devastating depression that had begun with the crash of the stock market in 1929. He won a decisive victory and immediately implemented his New Deal, a national program of economic reform and recovery. By the late 1930s, the country's financial situation had improved, and Roosevelt became increasingly popular with the American people.

During World War II, Roosevelt was a strong leader who effectively helped forge and maintain the Allied partnership against the Axis powers. He became known as a defender of democracy in the United States and around the world. And he bolstered people's courage during the most difficult days of the war by saying, "The only thing we have to fear is fear itself." Freedom-loving people around the world were stunned and saddened when Roosevelt died of a stroke in April 1945, shortly before the Allied victory he had worked so tirelessly to achieve.

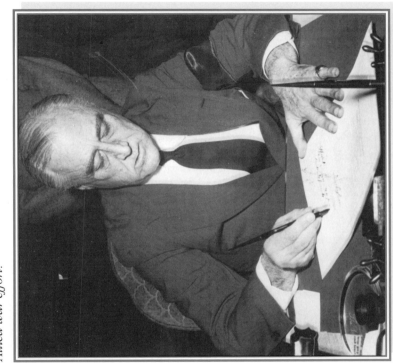

President Franklin D. Roosevelt signs a declaration of war against Japan. Congress voted to support Roosevelt and the Allied war effort.

Hideki Tojo

For Americans during World War II, Hideki Tojo (1884–1948) became a symbol of Japanese fanaticism and militarism. "Defeating Tojo" became synonymous with defeating Japan itself. Nicknamed the Razor by his supporters, Tojo was the son of a samurai. He was loyal to the ancient Japanese code of honor and believed that the Japanese were superior to other peoples. In the late 1930s, Tojo led a group

of Japanese militarists who wanted to see Japan aggressively expand into Asia and the Pacific. In 1940, he became war minister and in October 1941, premier of Japan. He had nearly total control of the Japanese war effort until his resignation in 1944. Captured by the Americans after the war, Tojo tried to commit hara-kiri but failed and was later executed for his role in waging the war.

Hideki Tojo was a fierce and ruthless Japanese military leader. He saw America as a threat to his country's expansionist goals.

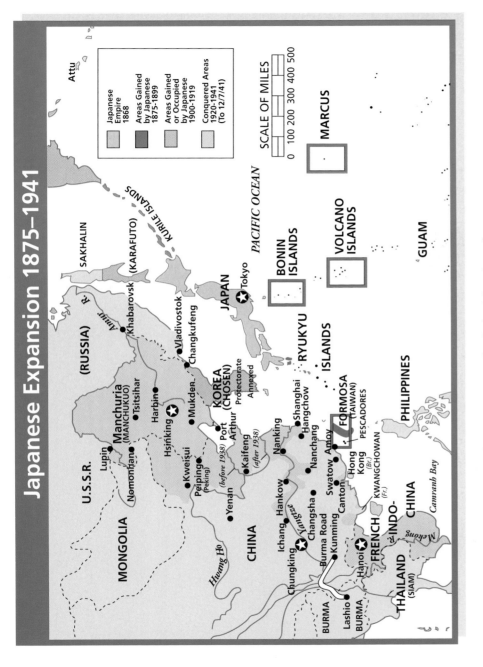

Japanese Expansion 1875–1941

Legend:
- Japanese Empire 1868
- Areas Gained by Japanese 1875–1899
- Areas Gained or Occupied by Japanese 1900–1919
- Conquered Areas 1920–1941 (To 12/7/41)

SCALE OF MILES
0 100 200 300 400 500

PACIFIC OCEAN

Attu
KURILE ISLANDS
SAKHALIN
(KARAFUTO)
MARCUS
BONIN ISLANDS
VOLCANO ISLANDS
GUAM
JAPAN
Tokyo
RYUKYU ISLANDS
Khabarovsk
Amur R.
Vladivostok
Changkufeng
(RUSSIA)
U.S.S.R.
Lupin
Nomonhan
MONGOLIA
Tsitsihar
Harbin
Manchuria (MANCHUKUO)
Hsinking
Mukden
Port Arthur
Peiping (Peking)
KOREA (CHOSEN)
Protectorate
Annexed
Kweisui
(before 1938)
Kaifeng (after 1938)
Yenan
Shanghai
Hangchow
Nanking
Nanchang
FORMOSA (TAIWAN)
PESCADORES
CHINA
Hwang Ho
Yangtze
Ichang Hankow
Changsha
Chungking
Burma Road
Kunming
Swatow Amoy
Canton
Hong Kong (Br.)
KWANGCHOWAN (Fr.)
PHILIPPINES
Hanoi
FRENCH INDO-CHINA
Mekong
Camranh Bay
THAILAND (SIAM)
BURMA
Lashio
BURMA

Americans felt that too many fellow citizens had died battling for foreign causes. The United States became so disillusioned by World War I that in 1928, American officials signed the Kellogg-Briand Pact, an international document condemning war as a means of national policy. As a result, during the period in which Japan moved from isolationism to expansionism, the United States followed nearly the opposite course.

By the late 1930s, Americans perceived that another war was brewing in Europe. They did not want to become involved. Between 1935 and 1937, Congress passed a series of neutrality laws aimed at keeping the country out of foreign wars.

Marching Toward War

In 1939, as many people in the United States had feared, war broke out in Europe. Adolf Hitler's deadly Nazi forces invaded Poland, shattering the peace of the world. With their German allies displaying such bold initiative, Japanese military leaders became more confident than ever about Japan's aggressive policies. In 1940, Hideki Tojo, a fanatic militarist, became Japan's war minister. Tojo strongly believed that the Japanese should live by the samurai code of honor. He insisted that non-Asian peoples like the Americans and British had no right to interfere with affairs in eastern Asia.

Shortly after taking power, Tojo and his followers announced the formation of the Greater East Asia Prosperity Sphere. Their slogan was "Asia for the Asiatics." Supposedly, the members of the sphere would be Asian peoples liberated by the Japanese from Western "bondage," but in reality, they were Japanese colonies taken by conquest.

Tojo and his supporters were convinced that the United States, with so many economic interests in the area, was the main stumbling block in their plans to take over most of the countries of eastern Asia and the Pacific region. Sooner or later, they believed, they would have to confront the United States. Japanese leaders made sure their people did not forget about how the Americans had humiliated Japan in the 1800s and referred to the United States as Japan's mortal enemy.

The confrontation between the two countries came much sooner than even Tojo expected. In July 1941, the Japanese marched troops into Indochina (now Vietnam) to seize the area's vast stretches of rice paddies, an important food resource for Japan's rapidly growing population. The American president, Franklin Delano Roosevelt, sternly warned the Japanese to get out. When they refused, he ordered that all Japanese money invested in American banks be "frozen." This meant that the Japanese could not use their own money to buy important supplies and armaments. Other countries followed Roosevelt's lead and froze Japanese investments. Enraged, Tojo and other Japanese leaders decided that there was only one way Japan could continue to survive and prosper. Japan must eliminate the United States as an economic and military threat. In the name of honor, Japan must attack.

In the following months, the United States continued to express its public opposition to Japanese aggression. But the Americans still hoped to avoid war and attempted to create a diplomatic solution. U.S. leaders had no way of knowing that the Japanese had already made up their minds to fight. Even while peace talks between the two countries were going on, the Japanese secretly assembled a huge fleet of seventy-two warships, carrying hundreds of planes and thousands of tons of bombs.

On November 26, 1941, this mighty armada sailed under the command of Adm. Chuichi Nagumo from Japan's Kuril Islands. Maintaining radio silence so as not to warn American planes and ships, the force headed for Hawaii's Pearl Harbor, where almost the entire U.S. Pacific fleet lay anchored. The plan seemed simple. The sons of the rising sun would destroy American military power in the Pacific in one bold stroke. Then, nothing could stand in the way of Japan's glorious dreams of conquest.

CHAPTER TWO

"Climb Mount Niitaka"— The Attack on Pearl Harbor

On Sunday morning, December 7, 1941, all but three of the huge warships of the U.S. Pacific fleet lay anchored in Pearl Harbor on the Hawaiian island of Oahu. The USS *Arizona, West Virginia, Oklahoma, California, Maryland,* and many other heavily armored vessels, along with smaller cruisers and destroyers, lined the docks of the harbor. Missing that fateful morning were the *Colorado,* in dry dock on the U.S. West Coast, and the aircraft carriers *Lexington* and *Enterprise,* which were at sea. Rows of military barracks, administrative and maintenance buildings, as well as civilian houses stretched along the coast to the harbor. Nearly four hundred American bombers and fighter planes were parked, wingtip to wingtip, on nearby airfields.

Unprepared for Trouble

By 7:00 A.M., some American personnel at the Pearl Harbor base were already eating breakfast or getting ready for church. But most were still asleep or lounging in their bunks. The general mood was calm because no one had any reason to suspect trouble. Everyone knew that American-Japanese relations had been strained since the Japanese invasion of Indochina the previous July. But Japan was thousands of miles away, and the Americans at Pearl Harbor assumed there would be weeks of advance notice if Hawaii were to be threatened.

At precisely 7:02, an Army Air Corps radar operator detected a large group of planes approaching Oahu from the north at a distance of about 137 miles. The operator quickly telephoned his

Minoru Genda—Master of Air Attack

When the Japanese admirals began to plot the attack on Pearl Harbor, they put Minoru Genda in charge of the planning. A thirty-six-year-old aviation expert, Genda had formerly served in the Japanese embassy in London. There, he carefully studied Great Britian's successful use of air power. Genda told the admirals that the Pearl Harbor plan, code-named Operation Z, was risky but still possible. He worked out the details with Mitsuo Fuchida, who actually led the attack. Later, Fuchida commented, "Genda wrote the script. My pilots and I produced it." Genda was able to coordinate a major air strike while maintaining complete radio silence. He remembered seeing a newsreel which showed four U.S. carriers moving together in close formation. The Americans signaled to each other using flags and spotlights. The Japanese, concluded Genda, could use these same tactics while launching planes against Pearl Harbor. In 1942, Genda planned the Japanese strategy for the Battle of Midway. He served his country again after the war as the head of the air force defense system from 1959 to 1962.

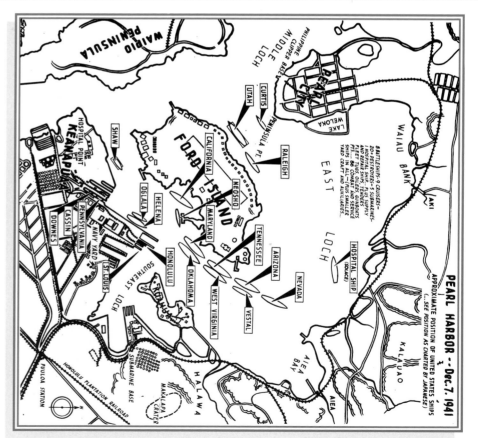

This map shows the approximate position of the United States' naval fleet at Pearl Harbor on December 7, 1941, the day Japanese pilots made a surprise attack there.

duty officer, Lt. Kermit Tyler. Tyler knew that a flight of American B-17 bombers had left California on December 6 and were due to arrive that morning on Oahu. Thinking that these were the planes that had been sighted, he told the radar man, "Don't worry about it."

What Tyler and his coworkers had no way of knowing was that the approaching planes were actually Japanese. The fighters had come to fulfill a top secret mission that Tojo and Japan's senior naval officers had planned in September. The pilots had been briefed on October 5 and had sailed, along with their planes, on the warships of Admiral Nagumo's mighty fleet. On December 5, at a secret rendezvous point in the Pacific Ocean north of Hawaii, the fleet received the coded radio message "Climb Mount Niitaka." This was the order to proceed with the surprise attack on the American base. Early in the morning of December 7, the Japanese planes lifted off their carriers and headed for Pearl Harbor.

The Japanese Attack Planes

During the 1920s and 1930s, the Japanese built one of the most modern and effective air forces in the world. U.S. aviation experts knew that the Japanese were building large numbers of planes. But the Americans greatly underestimated the worth of Japanese attack planes. U.S. officials thought the Japanese planes were poor copies of American planes. Said a U.S. military expert in 1938, "The [Japanese] ability to produce original [aircraft] designs is lacking." When the war began, the Americans were stunned by the superiority of Japanese warplanes.

Of the many types of fighter aircraft the Japanese designed, the world famous Zero was the most formidable. The Zero, which first saw service in 1940, was the first carrier-based fighter plane that could perform as well as land-based planes. It could fly at 330 mph, making it the fastest attack plane in the world when it was built. With its speed, superior firepower, and an ability to climb quickly and maneuver easily, the Zero was much more effective than any of the American planes during the early days of the war. Its one weakness was that it was constructed of lightweight materials and had no armor. This meant that even a minor hit could destroy it. Although American planes eventually surpassed it in speed and firepower, for at least two years, the Zero was the terror of the Pacific skies.

Other effective Japanese attack planes were the AICHI Type 99 Carrier Bomber, nicknamed the "Val" by the Allies, and the B5N2 Type 97 Carrier Bomber, nicknamed the "Kate." The Val flew at 240 mph, much slower than the Zero, but maneuvered unusually well. Vals sank more Allied warships than any other Axis planes during World War II. The Kates were deadly torpedo planes, each of which could carry a 1,764-pound torpedo. When one of these powerful bombs struck an Allied ship in the right place, the vessel was doomed.

The Japanese Zero fighter plane was a feared component of Japan's air force.

The Sinking of the Arizona

On the morning of December 7, 1941, the great battleship USS *Arizona* floated beside its sister ships of the Pacific fleet in Pearl Harbor, Hawaii. Ensign G.S. Flannigan remembered how an air raid siren suddenly broke the morning calm. "I was in the bunk room," recalled Flannigan, "and everyone thought it was a joke to have an air raid on Sunday. Then I heard an explosion." Within minutes, dozens of Japanese planes homed in on the *Arizona* and released a deadly rain of bombs and torpedoes. One bomb fell directly into one of the vessel's funnels. Seconds later,

the ship's "forward magazines blew up with a tremendous explosion and large sheets of flame shot skyward," according to one eyewitness. Burning debris from this blast landed on the nearby USS *Tennessee*, and ignited raging fires. More than twelve hundred of the *Arizona*'s crew, including Adm. Isaac C. Kidd, died in the attack. The ship went down, forever entombing many of the victims at the bottom of the harbor. After the war, a monument was erected atop the *Arizona*'s sunken bridge in honor of those who lost their lives.

Japanese bombs and torpedoes destroyed the USS Arizona, killing more than twelve hundred crewmen.

Mitsuo Fuchida, commander and leader of the attackers, flew ahead of the other planes to scout the target. He arrived high over Oahu at 7:53 A.M. and saw the American ships lined up like sitting ducks below. Excitedly, he radioed back to the other planes, "Tora! Tora! Tora!" (Tiger! Tiger! Tiger!), which signified the successful achievement of complete surprise.

A Wave of Destruction

At 8:10 A.M., a huge squadron of 189 Japanese planes swarmed like angry hornets over Oahu's volcano, Diamond Head, and swooped down on the unsuspecting Americans. Torpedo planes and dive-bombers began raining explosives on the warships in the harbor, while fighter planes attacked the airfields. Startled American sailors, marines, and other personnel scrambled to mount a defense, but they were hindered by deafening noise, smoke, flames, and mass confusion. The Japanese attackers roamed at will, blowing up barracks, hangars, and houses as well as ships and planes. They spread a wave of destruction as they went.

American admiral Husband E. Kimmel was in his home on a hill overlooking the harbor when he received the message, "The Japanese are attacking Pearl Harbor, and this is no drill!" Kimmel ran into his garden and watched helplessly as, one by one, the American warships were struck by bombs. The *Arizona* took a hit in its forward section and burst into flames. Like sharks sensing spilled blood, more Japanese fighters closed in and rained a barrage of bombs on the ship. As it sunk, more than twelve hundred of its crew of fifteen hundred died in the explosions and fires or drowned.

Massive explosions repeatedly rocked the other ships. U.S. commander Jesse Kenworth, serving aboard the *West Virginia*, recalled:

As I reached the upper deck, I felt a very heavy shock and heard a loud explosion and the ship immediately began to list to port. Oil and water descended on the deck and by the time I had reached the boat deck, the shock of two more explosions on the port side was felt. As I attempted to get to the Conning Tower over decks slippery with oil ... I felt the shock of another heavy explosion.

The *Oklahoma* was hit by three torpedoes and quickly capsized, taking four hundred men to their death. The *California, Maryland, Tennessee,* and many other ships sustained heavy damage and numerous casualties. Many sailors jumped from their sinking ships in desperation, only to be burned to death in a mass of blazing oil that covered the surface of the harbor.

Meanwhile, the relentless attackers destroyed nearly all the planes on the airfields, making it impossible for the Americans to

American ships and planes were virtually defenseless during the Japanese attack at Pearl Harbor.

muster a counterattack. The flight of B-17s that Lieutenant Tyler had confused with the enemy planes arrived at the height of the attack, but they carried no ammunition and could do nothing to help. Shot at by Japanese fighter planes, the B-17s barely managed to land on the badly damaged airfields.

The Bodies of the Dead and Dying

At 8:30 A.M., the attackers had spent their ammunition and departed. Fearing that another attack was coming, the American defenders desperately raced to set up antiaircraft guns and other defenses. Their fears were confirmed when, at 9:00 A.M., a second wave of Japanese planes, consisting of 175 bombers and fighters, appeared and mercilessly resumed the assault. The *Pennsylvania, Cassin, Downes, Shaw,* and several other American ships suffered damage. Some of the attackers flew low and fired at people running along the ground.

When the Japanese finally withdrew at about 10:00 A.M., Mitsuo Fuchida continued to circle overhead, photographing the results of the raid. "A warm feeling came," he later said, "with the realization that the reward [of all the planning and training]…was unfolded before my eyes." He took pictures for nearly an hour, then turned north toward the waiting Japanese fleet.

News of the Japanese attack shocked and outraged most Americans. U.S. citizens nationwide demanded immediate retaliation.

The Revisionist View of Pearl Harbor

At the end of World War II, a debate began among politicians, journalists, and historians about the circumstances of the U.S. entry into the war. The official view was that President Roosevelt had done everything in his power to avoid war and was as surprised as everyone else when the Japanese bombed Pearl Harbor.

Some people, however, offered a revised version of the events, saying that Roosevelt and his advisers wanted the Japanese to attack in order to give the United States an excuse for entering the war. Some revisionists said that Roosevelt expected Pearl Harbor to be bombed but purposely refrained from issuing a red alert to U.S. Pacific forces. Writing for the *Wall Street Journal*, William Chamberlain charged, "Like the Roman God Janus, Roosevelt…had two faces…for the public record…his first concern

was to keep the country out of war. But in more intimate surroundings…[Roosevelt] assumed that America was already involved in war." According to this view, Roosevelt hoped that wartime industrial production would help the country's economy. Supposedly, he also sought to bolster his own image as a world leader.

But most government officials and historians disagreed with the revisionist view. They stood by the findings of a congressional committee that looked into the matter. The committee found that there was "no evidence to support the charges…. On the contrary, all evidence conclusively points to the fact that they [Roosevelt and his advisers] discharged their responsibilities with distinction…and in keeping with the highest traditions of our…foreign policy."

View of Pearl Harbor during the attack. In the background is battleship row where the burning and damaged ships were harbored. Some revisionists believe Roosevelt allowed Pearl Harbor to be attacked.

Fuchida and his pilots left behind a scene of utter devastation. The base at Pearl Harbor lay in ruins. Giant columns of black smoke billowed from the twisted hulks of the crippled ships, and the bodies of dead and dying sailors floated in the water and littered the docks. Eighteen ships were sunk or badly damaged, and 308 planes were destroyed or put out of action. The human toll: 2,343 Americans dead, 1,272 wounded, and almost 1,000 missing. Half of the entire U.S. Navy had been wiped out, and American military power in the Pacific was effectively paralyzed. In stunning contrast, the Japanese lost a mere 29 planes. Their victory was complete and decisive.

Shock and Outrage

When the news of the Pearl Harbor attack reached Japan, the Japanese people celebrated joyously. The *Japan Times and Advertiser* ran the headline: "U.S. Pacific Fleet Is Wiped Out!" The paper went on to describe the triumphant attack and claimed that Japan had "reduced the U.S. to a third-class power overnight." Tojo went on the radio to announce the commencement of war with the United States. Afterward, a Japanese choir sang a patriotic song that included the lines: "Across the sea, corpses in the water, Across the mountain, corpses in the field."

In the United States, there was only shock and outrage. One American newspaper reported, "The U.S. Navy was caught with its pants down." Within hours, demands for retaliation issued from every corner of the country. Montana senator Burton K. Wheeler exclaimed, "The only thing to do now is lick the hell out of them!"

On Sunday afternoon, only hours after the destruction of the American fleet, President Roosevelt met with his military advisers. They received reports that the Japanese had also attacked the Pacific islands of Guam and Wake as well as British bases in Hong Kong, Singapore, and many other areas in Southeast Asia.

The next day, December 8, at 12:30 P.M., Roosevelt stood before a packed joint session of Congress and delivered his war declaration. His words went out over the radio to millions of Americans and listeners in other countries. He said, "Yesterday, December 7, 1941, a date which will live in infamy, the United States was suddenly and deliberately attacked by the naval and air forces of the Empire of Japan." Ending his speech with a dramatic call for a massive war effort against Japan, Roosevelt received a thunderous ovation of clapping and cheers. Without a single word of debate, Congress voted nearly unanimously to declare war.

Within hours, all political factions in the country, which usually bickered among themselves, put aside their differences. In a remarkable show of national unity, Americans from all walks of

British prime minister Winston Churchill also declared war on Japan.

life angrily opposed the Japanese. Even the famous aviator Charles Lindbergh, a staunch isolationist, lent his support to the war effort, declaring: "Now it has come, and we must meet it as united Americans regardless of our attitude in the past toward the policy our government has followed.... We must now turn every effort to building the greatest and most efficient Army, Navy, and Air Force in the world."

The World Goes to War

As war fever spread across the United States, the country's allies, many of them also victims of the Japanese attacks of December 7, declared war on Japan. Great Britain's prime minister, Winston Churchill, told Parliament: "Now that the issue is joined, it only remains for the two great democracies to face their task with whatever strength God may give them.... We have at least four-fifths of the population of the globe upon our side. We are responsible for their safety and for their future." Joining the United States and Great Britain against Japan were Canada; Australia; New Zealand; the exiled governments of Greece, Yugoslavia, and

France; and nine Latin American countries. These nations referred to themselves as the Allies. Predictably, the other Axis countries, Germany and Italy, backed Japan and declared war on the Allies.

The world was now engulfed in a state of total war. With such a formidable array of nations lined up against Japan, Tojo and his advisers had little time to assess the implications of their attack on Pearl Harbor. They just assumed that the humiliated Americans would not have the stomach to fight and that the U.S. military threat was eliminated once and for all. This, however, was a grave miscalculation. The Japanese had indeed dealt the United States a crippling blow at Pearl Harbor. But contrary to what the Japanese hoped and believed, the blow was not a fatal one.

And the attackers had made a number of serious mistakes. First, they failed to bomb the naval repair facilities at Pearl Harbor, so all but two of the damaged ships were quickly refloated and repaired. Second, the Japanese failed to find and destroy the carriers *Lexington* and *Enterprise* and their escort ships, which were at sea at the time of the attack. These ships, along with the fighter planes they carried, had the capability of inflicting heavy damage on the Japanese.

The most important mistake made by the Japanese leaders was their failure to realize the consequences of drawing the United States into the war. The Japanese did not take into account the overwhelming industrial might of the United States. Easy access to vast amounts of oil, coal, metals, and other natural resources essential in waging war meant that the United States would have a great advantage. The Japanese also failed to anticipate the tremendous food-producing capabilities of the United States and neglected to consider the unity and resolve of the American people during a national crisis.

While the Japanese underestimated the potential power of the United States, Winston Churchill did not. He had been hoping for the two long years his country had been fighting Germany that the United States would take Great Britain's side in the war. Churchill knew that once committed to the fighting, the United States would prove to be an incredibly powerful and virtually unstoppable force. Sooner or later, he declared, this force would turn the tide in the battle against the Axis nations. Churchill later wrote: "No American will think it wrong of me if I proclaim that to have the United States at our side was to me the greatest joy.... Hitler's fate was sealed.... [Italy's] fate was sealed. As for the Japanese, they would be ground to powder. All the rest was merely the proper application of overwhelming force."

CHAPTER THREE

From Batavia to Bataan—The Japanese Empire Expands

A t the beginning of the war in the Pacific, Japan enjoyed a brilliant period of expansion during which it encountered little significant resistance from the Allies. This was because the Allies were unprepared to wage war against Japan. The United States needed time to rebound from the attack on Pearl Harbor, to gear up its national war production and plan its strategy. Great Britain and several other European Allies were preoccupied with combatting Hitler and needed many more months to mount a second major offensive in the Pacific.

And so, the Japanese empire, called the "octopus" by many in the West, reached out to grab several prizes at once. Within days of the assault on the U.S. fleet on Oahu, the Japanese struck at the British colonies of Singapore, Malaya, and Hong Kong in Southeast Asia. Japanese troops poured southward from Indochina into Thailand. And Japanese planes bombed U.S. airfields in the Philippine Islands. At the same time, the Japanese navy took over the American-owned Guam, Wake, and other Pacific islands.

Crippling the British Navy

Perhaps the most dramatic and surprising incident of Japan's well-coordinated initial offensive was its attack on British naval power in the Far East. Based at Singapore, the thirty-five-thousand-ton battleship *Prince of Wales* and the thirty-two-thousand battle cruiser *Repulse* were stationed to protect British colonies in the area. When the Japanese struck locations all over

Japanese bombs and torpedoes sank the British battleship Prince of Wales, *shown here stationed in Singapore.*

Southeast Asia, British admiral Sir Tom Phillips decided to take the huge vessels to sea and try to destroy Japanese ships in the vicinity. But this proved to be a fatal mistake, for the British ships had no planes to provide protection from the Japanese air force.

On December 9, 1941, Japanese planes spotted the *Prince of Wales* and *Repulse* and sank them under a massive barrage of bombs and torpedoes. This shocked the Allies for two reasons. First, the tragedy left most of Southeast Asia defenseless, ensuring that the Japanese would conquer most of the area. Second, the incident called into question the effectiveness of large battleships, which had been the mainstay of the world's navies for decades. The sinking of the two giant vessels marked the first time that aircraft alone had sunk ships so large on the open ocean.

Following the elimination of British naval resistance, the Japanese grew even more confident. The Japanese octopus continued to reach out on the land and in the air, striking at strategic points in Asia and taking island after island in the Pacific.

One key to the entire Japanese offensive was the unusual effectiveness of Japanese fighting men. These troops were highly trained and disciplined. They knew how to survive for extended periods on small rations of rice and could live off the land if necessary. They learned to camouflage themselves to blend in with leaves and underbrush so they could creep unseen through the

Britain's Repulse (above) went to sea with the Prince of Wales to battle Japanese ships. Both ships were unprotected against enemy aircraft fire and sank.

jungle, and they often used animal cries to signal each other. And they were taught to follow the samurai code, choosing to fight to the death rather than surrender. All of these factors made Japanese soldiers extremely fearsome and formidable opponents for American and Allied troops.

The Conquest of the Philippines

One of the first major tests for the well-trained Japanese ground fighters was in the Philippines. The Japanese leaders knew that capturing the Philippines, a group of some 7,083 islands controlled by the United States, was essential to winning the war. This was because the Philippines extended for 1,150 miles along the strategic military and trade routes between Japan and southern Asia. Conquering the Philippines would practically ensure control of the valuable oil and mineral deposits of the Dutch island of Java and Malaya to the west and of the lands of China and Burma to the north.

On December 8, 1941, the Japanese attacked U.S. planes parked on runways at Clark Field near Manila, the Philippine capital. This and other similar raids destroyed most of the U.S. air power in the area. In the following three weeks, Japanese troops landed in seven different spots on Luzon, the largest of the Philippine islands, and quickly drove back the unprepared American defenders. The commander of the American-Filipino forces, Gen. Douglas MacArthur, sent a damage report to Washington on December 27: "Enemy penetration in the Philippines resulted from our weakness on the sea and in the air.... Lack of airfields for modern planes prevented defensive [moves]...and lack of pursuit planes permitted unhindered day bombardment. The enemy has had utter freedom of naval and air movement."

As the Japanese closed in on Manila, American troops evacuated the city, and thousands of Filipinos fled into the hills. Japanese planes then bombed the city, touching off massive fires. A few days later, Japanese troops moved in and took control. Immediately, they instituted the code of Bushido, a set of strict rules the Japanese would later impose on all the peoples they conquered. The code warned, "Anyone who inflicts, or attempts to inflict, an injury upon Japanese soldiers, shall be shot to death. If the assailant, or attempted assailant, cannot be found, we will hold ten influential people who are in or about the streets of municipal cities where the event happened." The iron hand of Japanese colonial rule tightened its grip upon the Philippines.

Japanese bombing raids left downtown Manila in ruins. Japanese troops took control of the Philippine capital soon after this photograph was taken.

Gen. Douglas MacArthur

Often referred to as the American Caesar, Douglas MacArthur (1880–1964) was one of the most important and talked-about leaders of World War II. He graduated first in his class at West Point in 1903 and was wounded and decorated in 1917 during World War I. Appointed to command the U.S. military in the Philippines in 1935, MacArthur gained world attention during the heroic defense of the islands from 1941 to 1942.

Later, in 1945, MacArthur accepted the surrender of the Japanese and became the supreme commander for the Allied powers in Japan. He oversaw Japan's rapid reconstruction between 1945 and 1951, then went on to lead the American forces in the Korean War.

Gen. Douglas MacArthur was a respected military leader. Before leaving the Philippines, he promised to return to liberate it from the Japanese.

Although he sometimes proved himself a brilliant strategist, MacArthur was often described by his colleagues as temperamental, ambitious, overly dramatic, and conceited. Believing that his opinions should never be questioned, he regularly argued with his advisers and even his superiors. It was such a disagreement that led President Truman to fire him from his post in Korea in 1951. Always controversial, MacArthur divided the American public into those who hated him because he was power-hungry and self-centered and those who loved him as a larger-than-life national hero.

The Bataan Death March

When the American-Filipino garrison on Bataan surrendered in April 1942, the Japanese decided to march the seventy-six thousand prisoners to holding camps farther north. The treatment of the prisoners by their captors was one of the most shocking examples of senseless and inhuman brutality in the history of warfare. On April 11, the Japanese tied hundreds of Filipino officers to poles and mercilessly bayoneted them to death. Herded into columns, the Americans and other Filipinos had to march without water under the blazing tropical sun. Japanese guards beat the men with rifle butts as they walked. Those that fell and could not get up were bayoneted. Some had to dig their own graves, and when they were done, guards buried them alive. Guards also taunted the prisoners with food and water but never gave them any. Even men sick with malaria or hobbling on crutches were tortured and brutalized. After six terrible days, the rag-tag column reached the camps. More than twenty-two thousand prisoners died on the march, and thousands more perished from disease and lack of food in the following months.

Japanese soldiers celebrate a successful offensive at Bataan. Allied troops later confiscated this photograph from a Japanese soldier.

General MacArthur ordered his troops to retreat to the Bataan peninsula in western Luzon, where he hoped they could hold out against the Japanese until help arrived. The Japanese launched massive attacks on Bataan. Cut off from resupply, the American-Filipino forces ran out of food and had to eat dogs, iguana lizards, monkeys, and snakes as well as berries and roots from the jungle. Their supplies of medicine also ran out, and they suffered from diseases such as dysentery, malaria, and scurvy. Yet as the weeks dragged by, the demoralized Bataan defenders managed to fight on.

The Evacuation of MacArthur

On February 22, 1942, President Roosevelt made a painful decision. He saw that the American situation on Bataan was hopeless and felt it would be a disaster for the United States and Allies if General MacArthur, one of their most brilliant generals, fell into enemy hands. Roosevelt ordered a special group of commandos to evacuate MacArthur and his family in secrecy to Australia. Before leaving, MacArthur told the American general left in charge of U.S. forces, "Defend Bataan . . . [as best] as you can." If

Thirty Seconds over Tokyo—The Doolittle Raid

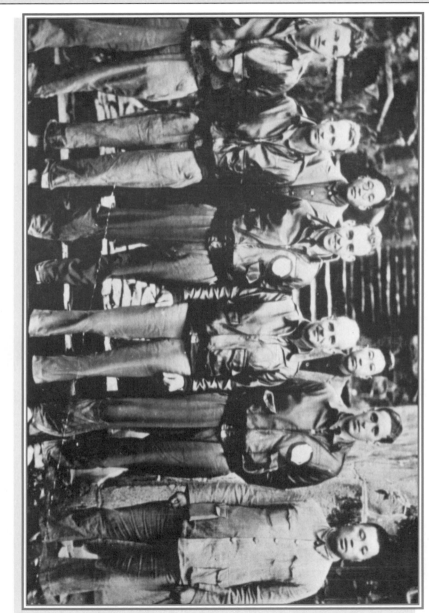

On April 18, 1942, the world was electrified with the news that a group of American planes had bombed Tokyo. This was the first significant incident of Allied retaliation against the Japanese in the war, and it filled the American people with pride and hope.

Shortly after the attack on Pearl Harbor, Col. James "Jimmy" Doolittle, a former stunt flyer, approached his superiors with a seemingly insane plan. He wanted to sneak a squadron of planes through the enemy's massive defense lines and bomb Tokyo. Military planners eventually agreed to the plan, hoping such a bold move would boost the morale of the country. After three months of rigorous, top secret training, sixteen B-25 bombers under Doolittle's command took off from the American carrier *Hornet*. They flew only a few feet above the waves in order to escape detection by enemy radar.

The Japanese in Tokyo were taken totally by surprise and could not mount an effective defense. During the thirty seconds the planes were actually above the city, they struck nearly every one of their planned targets with deadly precision. Plane factories, railroad yards, and a naval base were hit.

Although all the planes escaped, they later encountered a storm and ran out of gas. The crewmen had to bail out. Some were captured, but many made their way on foot to China and beyond. Eventually, seventy-one of the eighty airmen made it home. They had given their country the morale boost it needed and showed the Japanese that their own heartland was vulnerable at any time to American attack.

Col. James Doolittle (center) stands with part of his crew. The men bombed Tokyo five months after the war in the Pacific began.

Initial Japanese Offensives

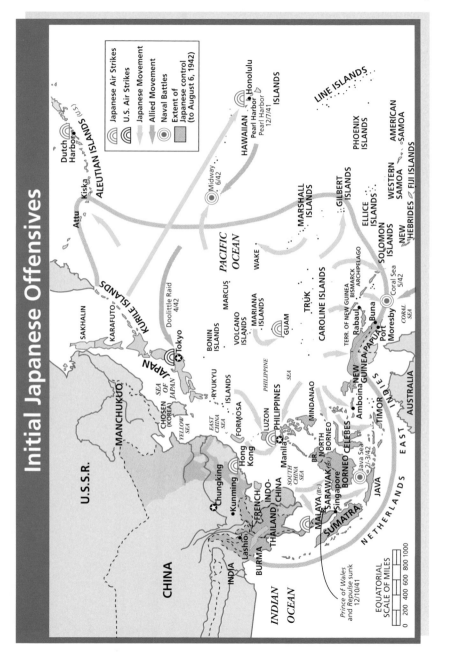

surrender becomes necessary, he said, "destroy as much [of your own materiel] as you can so that it cannot be used against an American effort to recapture the Philippines."

Indeed, the retaking of the Philippines became a major U.S. goal of the war and became MacArthur's responsibility. When he arrived in Australia, he told the world, "The President...ordered me to break through the Japanese lines...for the purpose...of organizing the American offensive against Japan, a primary purpose of which is the relief of the Philippines." In a stirring ending to the speech, MacArthur vowed to the people of the Philippines, "I shall return!"

On April 9, 1942, thirty-six thousand Americans and several thousand Filipinos on Bataan surrendered. Thousands of others managed to escape to Corregidor, a tiny island off the Luzon coast. The captured soldiers were forced on a bloody death march to prison camps in northern Luzon. The fifteen thousand Americans on Corregidor, heavily bombarded by Japanese artillery and torpedoes, were able to hold out until May 6, when they too were forced to surrender.

The conquest of the Philippines was a major triumph for the Japanese empire. For one thing, the loss of the islands was a massive and humiliating defeat for the Allies. More important, the Japanese now had Manila Harbor, one of the best in the world,

Adm. Isoroku Yamamoto

soroku Yamamoto (1884–1943), commander in chief of the Japanese navy, and one of the great military geniuses of World War II, grew up hating the United States. His father had told him bedtime stories about "the barbarians who came in their black ships" in the 1800s, "broke down the doors of Japan, threatened the Son of Heaven, and trampled the ancient customs."

To learn his enemy's weaknesses, Yamamoto traveled to the United States in the 1920s and studied at Harvard University. He quickly gained a healthy respect for the vast potential of American industrial and military might. He became convinced that fighting a conventional war with the United States and its allies would be a catastrophic mistake for Japan. For that

Japanese naval commander Isoroku Yamamoto suggested the attack on Pearl Harbor. Two years later, American pilots avenged the deed; they shot Yamamoto's plane out of the sky.

reason, when called upon to serve, he came up with the idea for the attack on Pearl Harbor, seeing it as the only way to eliminate the American naval threat.

On April 18, 1943, U.S. radio operators intercepted a secret message pinpointing the exact location of Yamamoto's personal plane. This was a stroke of luck for the Americans. Viewing Yamamoto as one of Japan's best military assets, they had wanted to eliminate him for some time but had never been able to find him. Ordered that they "must at all costs reach and destroy Yamamoto and his staff," sixteen U.S. planes attacked the admiral the next morning. In a matter of minutes, the Americans completed their mission, robbing the Japanese of their most brilliant strategist.

which they could use to supply their bases in Burma and Java. And the newly established Japanese bases in the Philippines could be used to launch attacks against the Allies all over Southeast Asia. Eventually, the Japanese hoped, the Philippines would become the staging area for an invasion of Australia.

Other strategic locales fell to Japan's overwhelming 1942 offensive. On February 27, the Japanese destroyed an entire fleet of American, British, and Dutch ships off the coast of Java and then invaded the island. By March 9, the attackers had taken control of the former Dutch colony, including its capital of Batavia, and had captured ninety-eight thousand Allied prisoners. After many weeks of bloody fighting, Burma, on the Asian mainland, fell to the Japanese in May 1942. Java and Burma were important prizes for Japan because they contained rich supplies of oil, rubber, metal ores, and foodstuffs. But the greatest prize of all would be Australia, the continent in the southern Pacific covering 2,974,581 square miles. Taking Australia, the Japanese believed, would completely demoralize the Allies. And then no one would be able to conquer Japan in the Pacific.

Japan's Zenith

As Japan's naval, air, and land forces ran wild in the Pacific, the United States could do little to check enemy advances. The Americans did engage the Japanese in a naval battle in the Coral Sea, north of Australia, in May 1942, but there were nearly equal losses on both sides. Apart from delaying the Japanese invasion of Australia, the confrontation was largely indecisive. By mid-1942, to the dismay of the Allies, the Japanese empire was at the height of its power.

The only moment of triumph for the United States in the early days of the war came in April 1942 when Col. James Doolittle led a brief raid of B-25 bombers over Tokyo, Japan's capital city and its largest. The move was designed mainly to boost the morale of the American troops and public. From a military standpoint, the raid inflicted relatively minor damage. It was a tiny foretaste of the massive U.S. counterattack to come.

But to the Japanese, the Doolittle attack was a humiliating stain on their country's honor. The Japanese militarists vowed to retaliate by destroying the remainder of the U.S. fleet. Gen. Isoroku Yamamoto engineered a plan to lure the Americans into a trap. If it worked, the U.S. West Coast would be left unguarded. The Japanese reasoned that a weakened and frightened America would then desire peace on any terms Japan dictated. Japanese admirals began to assemble the largest naval operation in Japanese history. Their target was Midway Island at the far western tip of the Hawaiian chain.

CHAPTER FOUR

Turning Point at Midway–The United States Strikes Back

n May 1942, the Japanese empire was enjoying its greatest expansion, while the Americans still attempted to recover from the disaster at Pearl Harbor. Each side knew that its number one priority must be to formulate an overall offensive strategy, a plan of attack against the other country. In creating a strategy, each side tried to guess the other's intentions. Military planners also took into consideration matters of national security and self-defense.

For instance, the Japanese strategy changed significantly in response to the Doolittle raid. Before the American strike on Tokyo in April, Japanese leaders were convinced that their country was well-protected, that no American planes would ever be able to penetrate Japan's defenses and threaten the homeland. The successful Doolittle mission showed the Japanese that their country was indeed exposed to destruction from the air. In particular, the life of Emperor Hirohito was at risk. This single fact so terrified the Japanese leaders that they vowed to make sure the country was well-defended. Never again, they said, would the American barbarians break through and bomb Japanese cities.

To war strategists in Tokyo, one dangerous hole in the Japanese defenses was Midway Island, at the tip of the Hawaiian Islands, about eleven hundred miles west of Oahu. Though only six miles in diameter, Midway was a key point in the American line of defense and was a gateway to the other Hawaiian islands. Admiral Yamamoto and his staff formulated Operation Mi, an attack on Midway. They hoped this move would destroy the remainder of the American fleet and eventually lead to control of the entire Hawaiian chain.

Cracking the Japanese Code

The Americans knew that they, too, needed a major victory. They realized that they must deliver a damaging blow to the Japanese navy in order to even the odds after the devastating losses at Pearl Harbor. But the Americans also realized that the Japanese now controlled most of the Pacific. Japanese ships moved constantly and swiftly from one strategic point to another. To have a chance at victory, the Americans had to be able to track Japanese ship movements and know their plans. To discover this information, the United States needed to break the Japanese secret military code.

Immediately after the attack on Pearl Harbor, a group of American cryptologists, experts at making and breaking complicated codes, set to work to crack the Japanese code. The group had its own secret code name—Hypo. By early April 1942, the Hypo experts were able to read 15 percent of the messages intercepted from the Japanese. Applying that knowledge to other portions of the Japanese code, the Americans could decipher 85 percent of the messages by early May. A few messages still could not be decoded, but the Hypo team members felt confident that they could make educated guesses about what they did not know.

American military success in the Pacific depended on breaking secret Japanese codes. U.S. cryptologists used decoding machines (below) and cipher disks (right) to decipher the complex messages.

A dramatic test for the Hypo unit came only days later. On May 12, the Americans decoded messages indicating that the Japanese would strike soon at the Hawaiian Islands. The messages referred to the target as "AF." But no one could figure out where AF was. Hypo captain Jasper Holmes devised a way to find out. He had the American base on Midway send out an uncoded message, a complaint that the base's water-purification plant had broken down. Within two days, Japanese signals flashed across the Pacific saying that "AF has problems with its water."

Holmes's trick worked, and the Americans now knew for sure that Midway would be the target. On May 20, other intercepted Japanese messages indicated the date and time of the attack. The Japanese would strike Alaska's Aleutian Islands on June 3 to confuse the Americans, then assault Midway the next day. Unknown to the Japanese, the Americans secretly prepared their forces for the coming battle.

The Deployment of the Fleets

The showdown between the Americans and Japanese at Midway was one of the most important and decisive naval battles in history. The Japanese assembled a gigantic fleet of more than 200 ships, including 11 battleships, 8 aircraft carriers, and 21 submarines. The carriers held more than 700 deadly fighter planes and bombers. By contrast, the Americans had only 70 ships, 3 of which were carriers, and about 350 planes, including those stationed on Midway itself.

Despite their numerical superiority in ships and planes, the Japanese made three serious errors. First, they expected the Americans to be surprised and unprepared. If the Americans had not known an attack was coming at Midway, their forces would have been too far away to stop the invasion. The Japanese did not know that the Americans had broken their code and therefore knew when and where the attack would come.

The second mistake the Japanese made was dividing their fleet into five separate units. These units were spread out over an area of several thousand square miles. This would make it difficult for the units to come to one another's aid. Each unit had a group of battleships and destroyers to protect its carriers from attack by American ships. If the Americans found and engaged one unit, the Japanese reasoned, the other four units could still take Midway and threaten Hawaii.

The third flaw in the Japanese plan was the assumption that the main American counterattack, if any, would come from battleships. This proved to be a grave miscalculation. The commander of the U.S. fleet, Adm. Chester W. Nimitz, believed that traditional naval strategy centering around battleships was outdated. Normally, the huge vessels moved close to an enemy fleet and blasted away with their big guns. But battleships presented easy

Japanese and American Propaganda Films

By the 1930s, film was a highly popular and influential form of mass communication. Millions of people around the world went to the movies on a regular basis, and the stories presented on the screen helped shape the way people saw their world. Naturally, government and military leaders of many nations were quick to use the cinema to mold public opinion. Propaganda films became a powerful weapon in the hands of moviemakers in the United States, Great Britain, Germany, Japan, and many other countries.

In the late 1930s, as Japan invaded China and threatened other areas of Southeast Asia, Japanese war films tended to emphasize personal stories of individual heroes. For instance, *Five Scouts* (1938), directed by Tomotaka Tasaka, depicted the trials of five young soldiers fighting in northern China. The style of the film was sentimental, focusing on the men's memories of home and family rather than glorifying war itself. Tasaka's *Mud and Soldiers* (1939) and Kimisaburo Yoshimura's *The Story of Tank Commander Nischizumi* (1940), also set in China, showed Japanese soldiers helping rather than exploiting the Chinese peasants.

In 1940, the Japanese government set up the Office of Public Information specifically to produce propaganda films. The tone of Japanese movies changed drastically. The films began to emphasize themes such as national loyalty and the invincibility of Japan. Most included long sequences of guns firing, soldiers marching, or bombs exploding, often accompanied by powerful classical music and heavenly choirs. *Capture of Burma* (1942), *The War at Sea from Hawaii to Malaya* (1942), and *The Suicide Troops of the Watchtower* (1942) were typical examples.

In the United States, which was the world's largest producer of motion pictures, the output

of war propaganda films was predictably heavy. Before the 1941 attack on Pearl Harbor, nearly all of the American war films depicted the fighting in Europe, showing the German and Italian dictators as cruel and corrupt.

After the United States went to war with Japan, anti-Japanese films appeared in two forms. First, there were highly polished documentary-style films that showed real news and battle footage and explained why it was important to defeat the enemy. The best and most famous of these were the *Why We Fight* films, directed by the famous Hollywood director Frank Capra, who headed the U.S. War Department Film Section at the time. Another Hollywood director, John Ford, made the powerful documentary films *The Battle of Midway* (1942) and *December 7th* (1943).

The other kind of propaganda film was the full-length Hollywood film, designed to entertain but also to arouse patriotism and build morale. *Bataan* (1943), with Robert Taylor, depicted the American defense of the Bataan peninsula, as did *So Proudly We Hail* (1943), with Claudette Colbert. *Guadalcanal Diary* (1943), based on the actual eyewitness accounts of Richard Tregaskis, told the stirring tale of Americans caught in the bloody jungle fighting north of Australia. Exploiting this film's propaganda potential, the War Department set up recruiting stations near theaters where it showed. Other notable patriotic American films of the war were *Thirty Seconds Over Tokyo* (1944), the story of the dramatic Doolittle raid, starring Spencer Tracy, and John Ford's *They Were Expendable* (1945), the story of the heroic service of the small torpedo boats based in the Philippines, starring John Wayne.

Adm. Chester W. Nimitz

A s commander in chief of the U.S. Pacific Fleet, Chester W. Nimitz (1885–1966) led his country's naval forces from the defeat at Pearl Harbor in 1941 to total victory over Japan in 1945. After attending the U.S. Naval Academy at Annapolis, Maryland, he served on submarines during World War I. In 1939, he headed the navy's Bureau of Navigation, taking on the role of commander in chief after the attack on Pearl Harbor. Nimitz was known for his organizational abilities and calm manner in times of danger. He oversaw the

team of admirals that won the battles of Midway (1942), the Solomon Islands (1942–1943), the Marshall Islands and the Philippines (1944), and Iwo Jima (1945). He correctly foresaw the end of traditional battleship strategy and recognized the importance of naval air power. Historian Samuel Morison said of Nimitz, "He had the capacity to organize…the leadership to weld his own subordinates into a great fighting team, the courage to take necessary risks, and the wisdom to select…the correct strategy to defeat Japan."

Adm. Chester W. Nimitz foresaw the end of traditional battleship strategy.

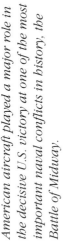

American aircraft played a major role in the decisive U.S. victory at one of the most important naval conflicts in history, the Battle of Midway.

The indecisiveness of Admiral Nagumo during the Battle of Midway cost the Japanese dearly.

targets for dive-bombers, and unlike aircraft carriers, they could not carry planes. Nimitz ordered American battleships to remain on the U.S. West Coast and built his plans around aircraft carriers. He would rely on his aircraft to strike quickly and cover great distances.

A Deadly Series of Delays

At 4:30 A.M. on the morning of June 4, 1942, the Japanese launched their attack on Midway as planned. Taking off from the carriers *Akagi, Kaga, Hiryu,* and *Soryu,* in the main force commanded by Admiral Nagumo, 108 planes assaulted the island's air base. Because the Americans knew the attack was coming, the base's planes made it into the air quickly and launched a counterstrike on Nagumo's ships. The planes did little damage but convinced Nagumo that he needed to launch a second strike against the Midway base in order to wipe out American resistance. He ordered another wave of bombers to be fitted with torpedoes for the attack.

Only a few hours later, at 7:30 A.M., Japanese planes spotted ten American warships just two hundred miles from Nagumo's fleet. Confused now about whether he should attack the island or the U.S. ships, the Japanese admiral hesitated. He waited to find out if the American fleet included an aircraft carrier. It was 8:20 before a Japanese pilot reported, "The enemy is accompanied by what appears to be a carrier." Knowing the danger posed by a carrier's planes, Nagumo decided to attack the ships.

At that moment, however, the Japanese planes that had struck Midway returned, needing to land on Nagumo's carriers. And his second wave of bombers was still waiting on deck to be fitted with torpedoes. This forced Nagumo to make further delays. All these delays proved to be fatal for the Japanese.

U.S. Planes Move In for the Kill

While Nagumo hesitated, U.S. commander Wade McClusky, leading a squadron of planes from the carrier *Enterprise*, spotted Nagumo's carriers. McClusky spread the word to the Americans.

During the Battle of Midway, U.S. Navy planes (above) attack the Japanese fleet. An enemy bomb explodes (right) on board the USS Enterprise. The blast killed the photographer who took this shot.

In less than an hour, wave after wave of American planes swooped down on the Japanese fleet. For the Japanese, this was the worst possible moment for an attack. Almost one hundred planes, still waiting to take off to bomb the Americans, lined the decks of the carriers. Each plane was loaded with bombs, torpedoes, and flammable fuel. Also stacked on the carrier decks were piles of torpedoes and other explosives.

As the American planes dive-bombed their targets, they touched off massive chain reactions of explosions, which turned the ships into floating torches. A sailor from the *Akagi* later recalled, "The terrifying scream of the dive-bombers reached me first, followed by the crashing explosion of a direct hit. There was a blinding flash and then a second explosion, much louder than the first." Another sailor aboard the *Akagi* remembered, "There was a huge hole in the flight deck.... Deck plates reeled upward in grotesque configurations. Planes stood tail up, belching livid flame and jet-black smoke."

As the American planes rained deadly bombs on Nagumo's ships, the American carriers *Hornet, Yorktown,* and *Enterprise* sent out second and third waves of aircraft. They scored repeated, devastating hits on the Japanese battleships and cruisers, which circled in a state of desperate confusion.

Hearing of the destruction of Nagumo's task force, Admiral Yamamoto called off the invasion and ordered the other four Japanese naval units to retreat. The entire U.S. fleet chased the enemy westward for more than two days, picking off more ships and planes. In the chaos of the retreat, two Japanese ships collided. American planes then moved in for the kill, sinking one ship and badly damaging the other. What was left of the Japanese fleet limped slowly away toward a humiliating homecoming in Japan.

The USS Yorktown *(left) sustained heavy damage during the Battle of Midway.*

The Strategic Importance of Midway

The encounter at Midway marked the first great turning point of the Pacific War. It was the first decisive defeat the Japanese navy had suffered in modern times. The Japanese lost more than 5,000 men, 4 aircraft carriers, several other ships, and 322 planes. American losses were much smaller: 307 men; 1 carrier, the *Yorktown*; and 147 planes.

The American victory did more than inflict heavy losses on the enemy. Forced to reshuffle their forces in the Pacific, the Japanese had to temporarily cancel their plans to invade Australia, New Zealand, and other areas. For the Americans, the defeat of the Japanese fleet ended all threats to the U.S. West Coast and put Japan on the defensive. The Japanese would now be confined to the southern Pacific and their own home waters.

The clash at Midway also proved that Nimitz had been right about the potential of naval air power. The battle marked the end of the traditional naval strategy centered around battleships with large guns. Surprisingly, the Japanese had not learned from their own earlier success—when the British warships *Prince of Wales* and *Repulse* had been helpless under Japanese air attack—that the key to modern war was air power. At Midway, none of the big warships exchanged fire; instead, the planes did all the fighting. In the future, all naval operations would be planned around the aircraft carriers.

The United States Mobilizes

Just as U.S. Pacific forces had mobilized to meet the Japanese at Midway, Americans at home marshaled their human and material resources for the war effort.

One of the first concerns of this mobilization was to ensure that national security was not threatened. Many in the United States were worried that Americans of Japanese ancestry, or AJAs, would sympathize with Japan and become spies against the United States. Giving in to the public's hysterical fears, the federal government ordered that Japanese-Americans be rounded up and sent to "relocation camps" in the western part of the country. Deprived of their property and freedom, most Japanese-Americans had to spend the remainder of the war behind barbed-wire fences.

Meanwhile, to boost the country's war economy, President Roosevelt and Congress instituted several important measures. First, on December 27, 1941, they set up a system of rationing. This meant that civilians could buy only limited amounts of many products, such as automobile tires, gasoline, shoes, sugar, coffee, and meat. Rationing allowed more of these items to be shipped to soldiers in Europe and the Pacific.

These wartime posters encourage U.S. citizens to keep all knowledge of the war secret. Many such posters were boldly racist, as caricatures in the top poster reveal.

The United States Imprisons Its Own Citizens

n the early months of World War II, the U.S. government imprisoned thousands of its own citizens in concentration camps. This action resulted from the unreasonable fear among many people that Americans of Japanese ancestry, or AJAs, might commit acts of treason against the United States. AJAs by the thousands were forcibly removed from their homes and taken to internment camps in central California, Nevada, and Utah. The government confiscated their property and businesses. The operation cruelly broke up many families, and some people died in the camps.

Those who supported the internment agreed with hysterical law enforcement officials who met in California in January 1942. One official said, "It is time for the people of California to disregard the law if necessary to secure their protection." Another official called for shooting all Japanese-Americans on sight.

Those against the action called it the most blatant mass violation of civil liberties in American history. They insisted that the internment was really motivated by ignorance and racism. They pointed out that the United States was also at war with Germany and Italy, but no Americans of German or Italian descent were interned.

The internment turned out to be both destructive and pointless. Many AJAs fought in the American army during the war, serving their country with great distinction and proving their loyalty. Many years after the war, some of the people who had been interned or had relatives who died in the camps sued the U.S. government. In the 1980s, the government finally admitted it had been wrong and agreed to pay the survivors money for their suffering. But many AJAs and other Americans felt that no amount of money could make up for the blind fear and hatred that had been directed at Japanese-Americans.

Because the federal government feared Japanese-Americans would spy for or sympathize with Japan, thousands of Japanese-Americans were sent to relocation camps during the war.

Most Americans were enthusiastic about the war effort and did what they could. They rationed food, recycled used goods, and declared their patriotism by joining the armed services or working in factories.

Millions of American women, most of whom had never worked outside the home, joined male workers in U.S. factories during the war. Consequently, America's war production was tremendous.

The war mobilization created more than material shortages in the United States. Sending millions of American men overseas created a huge labor shortage as well. To compensate, millions of women, most of whom had never before worked full-time outside the home, filled the many jobs in industry and business. In addition, on February 9, 1943, Roosevelt mandated a forty-eight-hour workweek, eight hours more than in prewar days. And a few months later, on June 25, Congress made labor strikes illegal in government-controlled plants. Both of these measures ensured that the output of war materials would not slow down.

This output was the most important aspect of the U.S. war mobilization. In 1942, in order to meet the threat from the Japanese in the Pacific, as well as from the other Axis nations in Europe, the United States embarked upon the greatest war production effort the world had ever seen. In an awesome display of industrial planning, tens of thousands of factories employing millions of workers operated twenty-four hours a day, seven days a week. The plants turned out weapons, clothes, food, and many other products.

Even more amazing was the speed with which American industry organized and expanded. Only one year after the bombing of Pearl Harbor, U.S. war production already equaled the entire industrial output of Japan, Germany, and Italy combined. And by 1943, production in the United States far surpassed that in the Axis countries.

American Women and the War Effort

When the Japanese attacked Pearl Harbor in 1941, the United States went from being a nation with high unemployment to one with a serious labor shortage overnight. More than ten million men entered the armed forces, leaving their normal jobs unfilled. At the time, only a small proportion of American women worked in full-time jobs outside the home, mainly because tradition dictated that women belonged at home taking care of children. The government now actively recruited women to fill men's jobs. Women even worked in occupations that involved hard labor and took jobs as brick masons, dockworkers, and metal riveters. Painter Norman Rockwell popularized the tough, capable, and proud Rosie the Riveter, who became a symbol of American women doing their part to help win the war. At the peak of wartime employment, 18,830,000 women of all ages worked at least twenty-five hours a week. Most of them put in well over forty hours a week.

Women also served in the military. In 1942, the government established the Women's Army Corps. Women who served in the corps were called Wacs. Women who served in the navy, marines, or Coast Guard were known as Waves. More than 100,000 American women served in the armed forces during the war. At first,

Female students at a Florida vocational school learn welding techniques.

These women affix airplane components at a manufacturing plant in Los Angeles.

because of concerns for their safety, they were not allowed to serve outside the continental United States or aboard combat ships or planes. However, this restriction changed somewhat by the end of the war, when more than 5,000 women worked in administrative jobs on bases in the Pacific. The outstanding performance of women in both industry and the military helped win the war. It also became an important factor in changing social attitudes about women, eventually leading to their increased acceptance in the workplace.

Women helped wartime production reach an all-time high. Here, a female worker checks one-thousand-pound bomb casings before they are filled with explosives.

The amount of materials the United States produced was staggering. The country became the world's leading shipbuilding nation overnight. Reducing the amount of time needed to build a ship from thirty to seven weeks, and turning out ship parts on huge assembly lines, American workers produced thousands of vessels a year. Between 1942 and 1945, the United States turned out 296,601 planes, 87,000 tanks, 2,434,553 trucks, and 17,400,000 rifles. In addition, American farms produced hundreds of millions of tons of beef, chicken, potatoes, dairy products, grains, and other foodstuffs for the country, its soldiers, and its allies. A large proportion of the total goods turned out went to Great Britain, the Soviet Union, and other countries fighting with the United States against the Axis powers. Historian Louis L. Snyder asserted, "The Axis was literally engulfed under a sea of American war production."

Dismembering the Octopus

Following the U.S. victory at Midway, the mounting flood of ships, planes, guns, and other armaments produced by American factories began to pour into the Pacific. In the face of mounting Allied strength, Japanese forces in the Pacific went on the defensive.

The United States wasted no time in following up its victory at Midway. While convoying masses of war materials across the ocean, the Americans attacked the Japanese at the island of Guadalcanal, several hundred miles northeast of Australia, in August 1942. The fighting on Guadalcanal lasted six months. The

Americans manufactured nearly 300,000 planes during the war.

Courage from Down Under

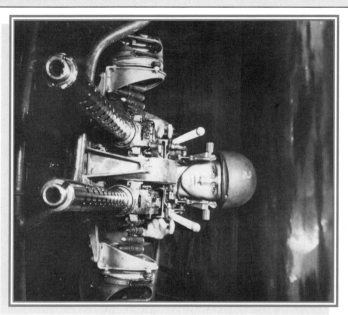

The fighting on New Guinea between Australian and Japanese soldiers was fierce and bloody. Here, an Allied marksman on board a ship off the New Guinea coast prepares to fire a double-barrel, fifty-caliber machine gun.

S ome of the bloodiest land fighting of World War II occurred when the Japanese and Australians engaged each other in fierce jungle fighting. In July 1942, the Japanese landed a force of more than fifteen thousand troops on the northern coast of the Australian-held island of New Guinea, just north of Australia. The Japanese goal was to trek through one hundred miles of mountains and jungle to the southern coast of the island and capture the city of Port Moresby. The Australians believed this city was essential to the security of their own country.

At first, the Japanese advance was successful. But in late August, the Australians, who were outnumbered by seven to one, staged a daring counterattack. Soldiers savagely fought each other in hand-to-hand combat for days.

Before the Japanese retreated to New Guinea's northern coast, the fighting was long and violent. These cameramen follow Australian troops to record the fighting against the Japanese.

Among the numerous examples of personal heroism is the story of Australian corporal Charles McCallum, who single-handedly beat back an enemy attack and killed forty Japanese fighters.

As the fighting dragged on into September and October, survival in the jungle became a nightmare. Disease took its toll, killing many on both sides. Starving Japanese soldiers died from eating spoiled food. Some even resorted to cannibalism and devoured the bodies of Australian prisoners. Eventually, the Japanese retreated to the northern coast. There, the Australians, now heavily reinforced, cornered and slaughtered the enemy in a series of merciless attacks. On January 2, 1943, the fighting finally ended, with only 350 of the original 15,000 Japanese invaders left alive. The Australians had given the proud Japanese army its first land defeat ever.

Americans and Australians joined forces on Guadalcanal, an island northeast of Australia, to fight the Japanese. Here, a U.S. Marine tank unit moves through the jungle.

battles on land, sea, and in the air were fierce and bloody. Samuel Morison, who took part in the struggle, recalled the "desperate fights in the air, furious night naval battles, frantic work at supply and construction, savage fighting in the sodden jungles, nights broken by screaming bombs and deafening explosions." By February 1943, the Americans, supported by heroic actions from the Australians, had managed to drive the Japanese from the islands directly north of Australia. The Japanese threat to the "land down under" was over.

The American leaders now saw the overall strategy they must use to win the war against Japan. Using its military and industrial might, the United States would bombard the enemy in wave after wave. Fighting to take back each of the conquered islands and territories, the United States would chop off the tentacles of the Japanese octopus one by one. The U.S. forces would relentlessly apply pressure, never stopping until they reached the very shores of the Japanese home islands.

CHAPTER FIVE

"In Death There Is Life"–
Japan's Desperate Defense

A s the United States relentlessly pushed the enemy westward toward their homeland, the Japanese forces desperately fought to hold their ground. But the Americans, aided by the British, Australians, and other Allied forces, methodically retook the Japanese-held islands and territories of the Pacific and Southeast Asia.

Facing increasingly overwhelming odds, many Japanese soldiers turned to the ancient samurai code to save their honor. Believing that dying in battle guaranteed them a place in heaven, they often charged fearlessly at American machine guns and artillery. When it came to a final decision between death and surrender, thousands of Japanese chose death. They were partly spurred on by propaganda issued by the Japanese government, which claimed that Americans were merciless barbarians who would destroy the Japanese home islands, rape Japanese women, and slaughter prisoners of war.

American soldiers found Japanese ideas about honor and death bizarre and often looked upon the enemy as having little respect for life. This image was reinforced by reports that the Japanese treated Allied prisoners of war inhumanely. Every American knew about the brutal Bataan death march and had heard stories of Japanese interrogation techniques. These included placing bamboo shoots under the fingernails of captured soldiers to make them reveal secret information.

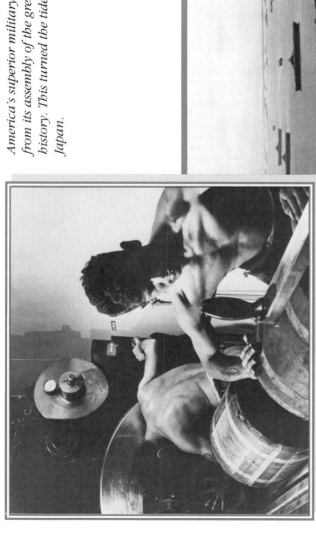

America's superior military strength resulted from its assembly of the greatest naval fleet in history. This turned the tide of war against Japan.

Superior Military Might

The Americans were able to keep the Japanese constantly on the defensive because of the vast superiority of American military might. Beginning late in 1942, the United States assembled the greatest concentration of naval strength in world history in the Pacific. By 1944, that military force was three times larger than Great Britain's and at least five times larger than Japan's. Most significant was that the number of aircraft carriers increased from three to more than one hundred by late 1944. Admiral Nimitz made sure that each of his large warships was accompanied by a repair ship so that damaged vessels did not have to travel to distant bases for restoration.

The United States also invented several new kinds of landing craft for assaults on the small Pacific islands. After ships and carrier planes bombarded a Japanese-held island, the landers swept ashore and discharged assault troops, guns, and supplies.

As soon as these forces took control of a section of an island, the landers brought in special engineers called Seabees. Most of the islands taken had few roads or airfields, and many of the existing structures had been damaged in battle. The Seabees

Once Americans gained control of an island, they would turn it into a new supply base and prepare to conquer the next island.

quickly built roads, docks, bridges, and airfields. Once an island had been taken from the Japanese, it became a new American supply base, a stepping-stone in the unrelenting Allied march toward the Japanese homeland.

The U.S.-Allied Offensive

The Allies pounded Japanese strongholds into submission, racking up one hard-won victory after another. After taking Guadalcanal in early 1943, the Americans assaulted the nearby Russell Islands and then the Solomon chain, all north of Australia. Meanwhile, the Australians, aided by American forces under General MacArthur, secured the large island of New Guinea. The Japanese attempted to reinforce these areas, sending a convoy of twenty-two ships and twenty thousand men. On March 1, 1943, U.S. planes spotted the convoy north of New Guinea and demolished it. The Americans also retook the Gilbert, Marshall, and Caroline island chains in the mid-Pacific by February 1944.

Reaching the Mariana Islands, less than twelve hundred miles south of Japan, in mid-1944, the Americans met especially heavy resistance. On June 19, the Japanese tried to halt the American advance by attacking with a huge fleet of carriers and destroyers.

Carnage on Saipan

The rash of wartime Japanese suicides reached a dramatic and grisly climax when U.S. troops attacked the tiny island of Saipan in the Marianas in June 1944. As the Americans fought their way across the island, the Japanese countered with numerous charges, hurling themselves in waves at U.S. machine guns and screaming "Banzai!" The largest such charge of the war occurred on Saipan on the night of July 6. More than three thousand Japanese, some with guns and bayonets, but many with no weapons at all, ran headlong at the amazed American troops. Many Americans died in the wild assault before all the attackers were killed. Several Japanese officers, including the famous Admiral Nagumo, then committed hara-kiri in nearby caves.

A few days later, these horrors were overshadowed when hundreds of Japanese civilians gathered at the island's northern cliffs. They were terrified by propaganda stories about Americans brutalizing, raping, and killing prisoners. Rather than be captured, many parents threw their babies onto the rocks below, then jumped to their own deaths. Others cut each other's throats, drowned themselves, or blew themselves up with hand grenades. Unable to stop them, American soldiers could only watch in utter disgust and bewilderment.

Some of the fiercest fighting during the Pacific war occurred when U.S. Marines landed on the island of Saipan. Here, troops crouch under enemy fire.

After taking the beach at Saipan, American soldiers disembark from troop transports and wade to shore.

Communication was crucial (top) and fighting was fierce (middle, bottom) during the American campaign in early 1944 to liberate the Gilbert, Marshall, and Caroline island chains.

In what later became known as the Battle of the Philippine Sea, or the "great Marianas turkey shoot," U.S. planes shot down 315 of Japan's best planes and pilots and sank 3 Japanese carriers. Total U.S. losses: 23 planes. It was a crushing defeat for Japan. The Americans then assaulted each Mariana island, facing stubborn Japanese resistance. Rather than surrender, the defenders staged mass-suicide charges. Japanese soldiers, often carrying only swords, ran headlong at U.S. machine guns and artillery, forcing the Americans to kill them.

The Retaking of the Philippines

One of the most important U.S. goals was to drive Japanese forces from the Philippines, which was Japan's vital supply and communications link with Southeast Asia. The American strategy of leapfrogging from island to island across the Pacific had proved highly effective. Now, U.S. forces were poised to launch a major strike on Leyte Island in the central Philippines.

In mid-October 1944, a massive armada of 600 warships and 250,000 men approached the target. First, American planes attacked Japanese airfields up and down the Philippine coasts, destroying more than 3,000 enemy planes. On October 21, after bombers had weakened Japanese positions on Leyte, U.S. landing forces stormed ashore.

Only hours after the assault began, one landing craft came close to shore and discharged a tall man with a corncob pipe. This was Gen. Douglas MacArthur, fulfilling his promise to return and liberate the Philippines. He and his staff, accompanied by Gen. Carlos Romulo, the Filipino leader, waded proudly through the knee-deep water and onto the beach. In his first official statement, MacArthur announced, "People of the Philippines! I have returned. By the Grace of Almighty God our forces stand again

Philippine forces leader Gen. Carlos Romulo converses with an American admiral.

Gen. Douglas MacArthur (center) returns to the shore at Leyte, hours after the initial Philippine assault began.

on Philippine soil—soil consecrated in the blood of our two peoples.... Rally to me. Let the indomitable [unbeatable] spirit of Bataan and Corregidor lead us on."

As the American forces pushed inland on Leyte Island, the Japanese massed most of their remaining warships for a last desperate attempt to stop the invasion. Japanese strategists divided their force into three sections. The first would act as a decoy to lure the Americans away from the Leyte beachhead. Meanwhile, the other two sections of the fleet would sail around Leyte from the north and south and attack the U.S. fleet from the rear.

Guts, Gumption, and Victory at Sea

Occurring over the course of nearly four days, from October 23 to 25, 1944, the Battle of Leyte Gulf was the greatest sea battle ever fought. It began with the utter destruction of the southernmost Japanese fleet by an American force commanded by Rear Adm. Jesse B. Oldendorf. As the Japanese ships emerged from the Surigao Strait, south of Leyte, a waiting lineup of U.S. warships sank them one by one. Only one Japanese vessel survived. Oldendorf later said, "Never give a sucker a chance. If my

A burial at sea (left) follows the Battle of Leyte Gulf. Amphibious assault vehicles (below) motor toward the Leyte shore.

opponent is foolish enough to come at me with an inferior force, I'm certainly not going to give him an even break."

Meanwhile, the Japanese decoy ships had succeeded in drawing a large portion of the American fleet northward. This left a tiny group of U.S. ships under the command of Adm. C.A.F. Sprague to face the large remaining Japanese task force. A savage naval fight followed, which one American officer compared to "a puppy being smacked by a truck." Yet the greatly outnumbered American forces constantly attacked the Japanese. They weaved among the enemy ships, using hit-and-run tactics, valiantly keeping the Japanese away from the beaches. Although Sprague's ships sustained heavy damage, they managed to fight until the enemy withdrew. Samuel Morison commented, "In no engagement in its entire history has the United States Navy shown more gallantry, guts, and gumption."

The fighting in Leyte Gulf took its toll on both sides. The Americans lost one carrier, five other ships, and three thousand men. But the Japanese suffered a major defeat, losing four carriers, three battleships, nineteen destroyers, and some ten thousand men. The United States had effectively knocked the Japanese navy out of the war.

Still, the fighting in the Philippines dragged on for many months. On island after island, Japanese soldiers, with no hope of victory, forced the Americans to pay in blood for every square foot of territory. In July 1945, the battle for the Philippines finally ended. Japan had lost more than 400,000 of its best-trained fighting men. As for the Americans, they were back to stay. When MacArthur set foot on Corregidor, he ordered, "Hoist the colors and let no enemy ever haul them down."

Tightening the Noose Around Japan

With the Marianas and Philippines retaken and the Japanese navy nearly destroyed, Japan itself lay wide open to invasion by the Americans. The final assault called for a two-pronged offensive. First, U.S. forces would destroy Japanese merchant ships and cut supply lines by blockading Japan. The nation would then be isolated from its outside sources of oil, coal, iron, foodstuffs, and other essential commodities. In the first months of 1945, the United States reduced Japan's flow of incoming supplies to a trickle, and many people in Japan began to hoard coal, food, and other goods.

The second aspect of the U.S. offensive was the repeated and massive bombing of Japanese cities, military installations, and industrial facilities. The Americans dropped hundreds of thousands of tons of bombs on Japan. Many cities were leveled, including Tokyo, which burned almost to the ground on the night of March 9, 1945. U.S. Air Force commander Maj. Gen.

Once the Philippines were liberated, U.S. forces began bombing missions against Japan (above). These missions destroyed parts of Tokyo (left) and other Japanese cities.

George C. Kenney warned, "Japan must surrender or the United States will strike Japan with 5,000 planes a day and reduce the country to a nation of nomads."

The combined blockade and bombing effort created chaos in Japan. Most schools and other public institutions closed as millions of citizens fled from cities and towns into the countryside. With supplies dwindling and the country practically bankrupt, the Japanese people were suffering. Many began to ask if continued fighting was worth the price. But the Japanese militarists refused even to think about surrender. "One hundred million die together!" became their new catchphrase as they committed the nation to fight to the death. As an American historian put it, "Japan was on the verge of total collapse, but its leaders wanted to save face, so tragically the war continued."

Japan's Last-Ditch Defensive

In early 1945, the last two strategically important islands still held by the Japanese were Iwo Jima and Okinawa. Each was located only a few hundred miles south of Japan, and the Japanese considered them gateways to their homeland. So they transformed both islands into fortresses with huge concrete walls, fields of land mines, and networks of underground tunnels.

The Nightmare of Iwo Jima

Located only 750 miles southeast of Japan, Iwo Jima was one of the last stepping-stones in the American march toward the Japanese home islands. The Japanese had turned the tiny island of eight square miles into a nearly impregnable fortress. A defending force of twenty-one thousand men dug themselves in, vowing to fight to the death. They devised thousands of booby traps and carved eleven miles of tunnels and caves into the island's rocky, volcanic surface. The 550-foot Mount Suribachi on the southern end of the island was honeycombed with caves and holes that were perfect for snipers.

For seventy-five days, American planes pounded Iwo Jima with explosives, dropping more than forty thousand bombs in the last three days alone. Then, on February 19, 1945, thirty thousand marines swept ashore, and one of the bloodiest episodes in the history of warfare began. Japanese snipers hiding underground often waited until American soldiers were only a few feet away before they opened fire. The Americans countered with deadly hand-held and tank-mounted flamethrowers, which poured out streams of burning liquid. For days, hand-to-hand combat raged. Opponents used knives and bayonets when their bullets ran out. The attackers had to fight for every square foot, taking a full three days to capture a mere seven hundred yards of territory.

During the morning of February 23, a marine patrol fought its way to the summit of Mount Suribachi and raised the U.S. flag. Associated Press photographer Joe Rosenthal was with them, and he snapped the now world famous photo that immortalized that triumphant moment. But it took the Americans nearly another month to secure the entire island. The final death toll was grim: 6,821 Americans killed, almost 18,000 wounded, and nearly 21,000 Japanese killed. The scars of battle lingered. Maria Talen, a USO performer who entertained troops in the months following the battle, recalled that arms, heads, and other body parts continued to wash in with the tide. "There were rows of white crosses as far as the eye could see," she remembered, "and I wept at the overwhelming horror of it all."

Marines plant the American flag at the top of a hill on Iwo Jima, the site of some of the bloodiest fighting in the war. Once on Iwo Jima, U.S. forces were just 750 miles from Japan.

The Sinking of the *Yamato*

On April 6, 1945, in an attempt to meet the American threat on Okinawa, what remained of the Japanese fleet sailed from Japan. One of these vessels was the seventy-thousand-ton *Yamato*, the largest battleship ever built. Accompanying the *Yamato* was the cruiser *Yahagi* and an escort of eight destroyers. The next day, 386 U.S. planes found the Japanese ships and moved in for a deadly assault. Since all available Japanese planes were now being used by the kamikazes, the *Yamato* and its small escort vessels had no air cover. The ships were sitting ducks. The American planes attacked in three waves, scoring nearly twenty direct hits on the *Yamato*. Helldiver attack craft from the *U.S.S. Bennington* scored hits near *Yamato*'s large smokestack at 12:41 P.M. At 12:45, an American Avenger attack plane torpedoed the battleship's bow, opening a wide gash near the waterline. The Japanese fired back with every machine gun and anti-aircraft weapon aboard. But these defensive measures could not stop the savage American attack. The *Yamato* finally exploded in a gigantic fireball and sank, taking with it Japan's dreams of world conquest.

The final American offensive against the Japanese depended heavily on superior air power (top left), immediate care for wounded soldiers (top right), and a highly organized ground crew (above).

U.S. forces stormed Iwo Jima on February 19 and Okinawa on April 1, 1945. The fighting was the bloodiest of an already bloody war. The combat was savage and chaotic. Historian William Manchester, who fought at Okinawa, said later, "We were all psychotic [crazy], inmates of the greatest madhouse in history." The Japanese defenders fought relentlessly. A U.S. Marine described how, on Iwo Jima, his friend "found a seriously wounded Jap trying to get his heavy machine gun into action. He emptied his clip at him but the Jap kept reaching. Finally, out of ammunition, the Marine used his knife to kill him." In all, the Japanese lost more than 130,000 men defending the two islands. The victorious Americans lost more than 19,000.

As the Americans closed in on Japan, the Japanese chose military suicide as a last line of defense. The country's leaders called for the creation of special units of suicide pilots known as kamikazes. Japanese for "divine wind." These men believed that they would be honored in the afterlife after bravely dying for

Preparing for Death

Following the ancient military code of the samurai, which taught that surrender was the ultimate disgrace, the kamikaze pilots sacrificed their lives in daring suicide attacks against the United States. The name *kamikaze* came from the Japanese legend of the Divine Wind, which was sent by the sun-goddess to destroy the fleet of Mongol invaders in the thirteenth century.

Most of the kamikaze pilots were young, in their teens or early twenties, with barely the amount of training needed to fly their death missions. Before taking off, they celebrated by drinking toasts to the emperor, to the empire, and to the glory of death and the afterlife. Many sang the "Kamikaze Song of the Warrior," which

included the lines, "In serving on the seas, be a corpse saturated with water.… In serving in the sky, be a corpse that challenges the clouds. Let us all die close by the side of our royal leader."

Next, the pilots wrote their last letters to loved ones. "May our deaths," said one young man, "be as sudden and clean as the shattering of crystal." Another wrote, "We shall plunge into the enemy ships cherishing the conviction that Japan has been…a place where only lovely homes, brave women and beautiful friendships are allowed to exist." And another pilot begged, "Most important of all, do not weep for me." Finishing their letters, they marched with heads held high to their planes and flew away to certain death.

Japanese kamikaze pilots caused an inordinate amount of damage to U.S. and Allied warships. The pilots' desperate efforts, however, could not save Japan from eventual defeat.

The Tokyo Fire Storm

The most devastating U.S. bombing raid of the early months of 1945 occurred on the night of March 9. A huge squadron of 280 American bombers released more than two thousand tons of incendiary, or fire-producing, bombs on Tokyo, a city of two million people. A stiff breeze fanned the flames until a mighty fire storm developed. In a fire storm, the heat of the fires quickly rises and billows out, creating large air drafts that carry the flames along at forty or fifty miles an hour. In Tokyo, walls of fire swept across the city, destroying everyone

Incendiary bombs dropped by U.S. planes onto Tokyo and other Japanese cities took many lives and caused much damage.

and everything in their paths. An eyewitness remembered, "As I ran, I kept my eyes on the sky. It was like a fireworks display as the incendiaries exploded.... People were aflame, rolling and writhing in agony, screaming piteously for help, but beyond all mortal assistance." The fire storm, the glow of which could be seen for 150 miles, completely obliterated sixteen square miles of Tokyo. An estimated 200,000 people died. Most were charred to ashes, their identities forever erased.

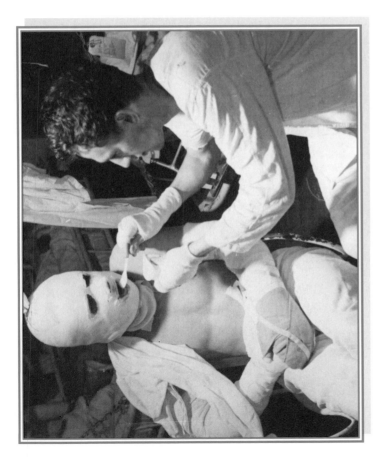

This American sailor's face and hands were burned after a kamikaze pilot crashed onto the deck of the USS Solace, a hospital ship.

their country. Thousands of them purposely crashed their aircraft, which were filled with explosives, into American ships. Often, trying to insult the enemy, they screamed "Babe Ruth, go to hell!" as they dived at their targets. Desperate U.S. gunners shot down many of the suicide planes, but many more fulfilled their mission. In all, the kamikazes sank 34 ships and damaged 288, including the mighty carrier *Enterprise.* But even the bloody sacrifices of Japan's young pilots were not enough to help the collapsing Japanese empire. Unable to match the might of the United States and other Allied nations, Japan's fate was sealed.

The Call for Japanese Surrender

On several occasions in early 1945, President Roosevelt called upon the Japanese to surrender. All of these demands were refused. Then, on April 12, 1945, at the height of the fighting in Okinawa, the world was shocked by the news that Roosevelt had died suddenly of a stroke. Winston Churchill lamented, "It is indeed a loss, a bitter loss to humanity, that those heartbeats are stilled forever." The same sentiments came from people in the United States. A New Yorker observed, "It is too bad ... this great man could not have carried his burden just a little while longer, to enjoy the peace he had won for us." Many felt that the spirit of the American war effort had died with Roosevelt. But another

U.S.-Allied Offensives Push Japan Westward

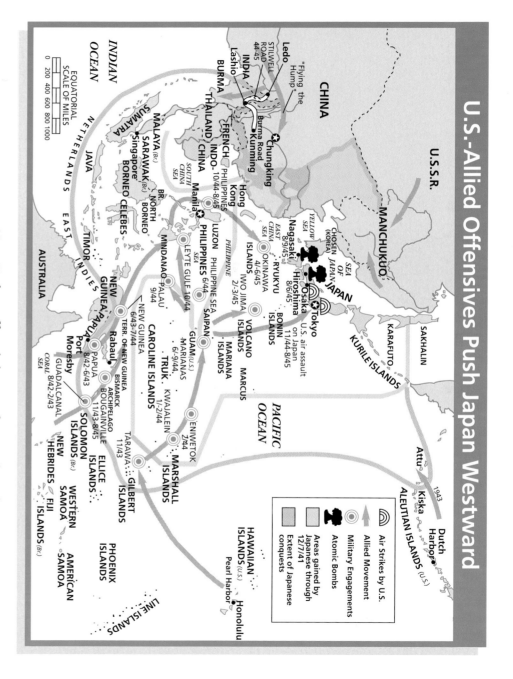

New Yorker offered the comforting thought, "Don't worry.... His plans are made and somebody's gonna carry them out."

That "somebody" was Harry S Truman, who was sworn in as the nation's thirty-third president only hours after Roosevelt's death. The job of finishing off Japan now belonged to Truman, who told the press, "I don't know if any of you fellows ever had a load of hay or a bull fall on him, but last night the whole weight of the moon and stars fell on me. I feel a tremendous responsibility. Please pray for me."

Truman, like Roosevelt, called for the Japanese to surrender unconditionally, which meant without receiving any special terms or deals. The Japanese militarists refused and continued their defiant stance. Even though their military was crippled and their economy devastated, they refused to give up. They believed that the Japanese people could withstand whatever the United States and the Allies could throw at them. They did not know, as Truman did, that throughout the war, American scientists had been developing a secret, unbelievably powerful weapon. That weapon had the strength to bring any nation to its knees. In the summer of 1945, it was ready for use.

CHAPTER SIX

Nuclear Dawn—
The United States Drops
the Atom Bomb

After the United States captured the Japanese stronghold of Okinawa in late June 1945, the Americans began preparations for the greatest undertaking of the war. Two sweeping military plans—Operation Olympic and Operation Coronet—would begin the massive invasion of the Japanese home islands. Kyushu, the southernmost large island in the group, would be the first major target. American planners expected that the assault would be time-consuming and bloody.

But the climactic invasion of Japan never occurred. Instead, the war came to an abrupt and decisive end in a way no one could have predicted. As soldiers died by the thousands on the beaches of Iwo Jima and Okinawa, American scientists secretly labored to put the finishing touches on the most terrifying weapon ever devised. Only a handful of Americans and Allied leaders knew that the scientists had been working on the device since 1939.

Birth of the Manhattan Project

The effort to develop an atomic bomb was code-named the Manhattan Project. It was the culmination of a series of important scientific discoveries made in the 1920s and 1930s. Researchers such as Albert Einstein, Danish physicist Niels Bohr, and British physicist Ernest Rutherford studied the structure and behavior of atoms, the tiny building blocks that make up all matter. Among other things, they recognized that splitting atoms of uranium and other radioactive elements released unusually large amounts of energy.

To escape Europe's Axis dictatorships, many of the world's leading atomic scientists, including Einstein, Bohr, and Italy's Enrico Fermi, moved to the United States in the late 1930s. There, they continued with their research into the splitting of the atom, called fission.

It did not take these scientists long to realize that the energy released during fission might be utilized in a weapon of enormous destructive power. The race to develop such a weapon began with a historic letter from Einstein to President Roosevelt on August 2, 1939. Einstein asserted:

It may become possible to set up a nuclear chain reaction in a large mass of uranium, by which vast amounts of power ... would be generated.... This new phenomenon would also lead to the construction of bombs.... A single bomb of this type, carried by boat and exploded in a port, might very well destroy the whole port, together with some of the surrounding territory.

Accepting Einstein's suggestion, Roosevelt and Winston Churchill immediately launched the huge and highly secret Manhattan Project. They felt there was good reason for haste. Allied spies reported that German scientists were also developing atomic bombs, which Hitler might use against Great Britain and eventually against the United States. This fear kept scientists working on the Manhattan Project at an ever-increasing pace. Many U.S. leaders also believed that the bomb was just what the country needed to quickly and decisively win the war.

Atomic scientists Enrico Fermi (left) and Niels Bohr researched the splitting of an atom, called nuclear fission.

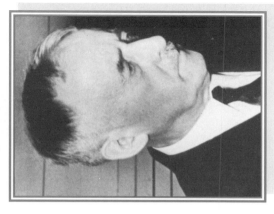

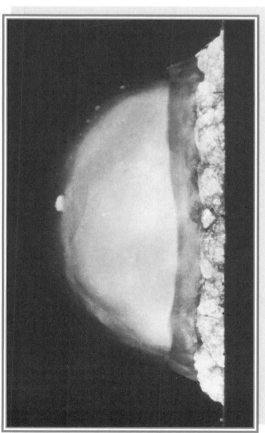

Dr. J. Robert Oppenheimer (below, top) directed the construction of the atom bomb. Secretary of War Henry L. Stimson (below, bottom) led the committee that decided how the bomb would be developed and delivered.

The development of the atom bomb caused the quick and decisive end of the war in the Pacific. Even though it caused untold devastation in human lives and suffering, many people believe the war would have continued much longer without its use.

The Roar That Warned of Doomsday

The Manhattan Project was the most complex and costly scientific endeavor in history. It ended up costing the United States and Great Britain $2.5 billion, a tremendous sum at the time. The project involved scientists, military personnel, and labs all over the United States. Henry L. Stimson, secretary of war, headed the president's committee that decided how the bomb would be developed and delivered. Dr. J. Robert Oppenheimer led the scientific team, and Maj. Gen. Leslie R. Groves commanded the Army Corps of Engineers, whose task was to build the device. The government built two huge plants for bomb construction. One was in Oak Ridge, Tennessee, the other in Richland, Washington. Oppenheimer and his team of scientists worked at a special lab at Los Alamos in the desert near Santa Fe, New Mexico.

Security was tight. Although more than 200,000 people helped produce the bomb, only a tiny handful knew what they were actually working on. Even Vice President Truman knew nothing of the project until he was sworn in to succeed Roosevelt in April 1945. Those in charge made sure that it was the "best-kept secret of the war."

The atomic age began on July 16, 1945, when Oppenheimer's and Groves's units conducted a test firing of the new superweapon in the desert near Alamogordo, New Mexico. Although most of those working on the project believed the device would work, no one was prepared for the awesome power the weapon actually possessed. The large steel tower that held the bomb was

How Atomic Fission Works

Fission occurs when a microscopic particle traveling at high speed strikes the nucleus, or center, of a large radioactive atom such as uranium 235. The nucleus splits and sends out more of these particles. These then hit other nearby atoms, splitting them apart, and the process quickly speeds up. Each time an atom splits, a small amount of energy is released as a by-product. As more and more atoms are split, a

chain reaction takes place and a huge amount of energy is generated in the form of heat and light.

An atom bomb works by forcing a mass of radioactive material to undergo an uncontrolled chain reaction. The potential energy locked within atoms is so great that a mass of fission-able material weighing only a few pounds can destroy an entire city.

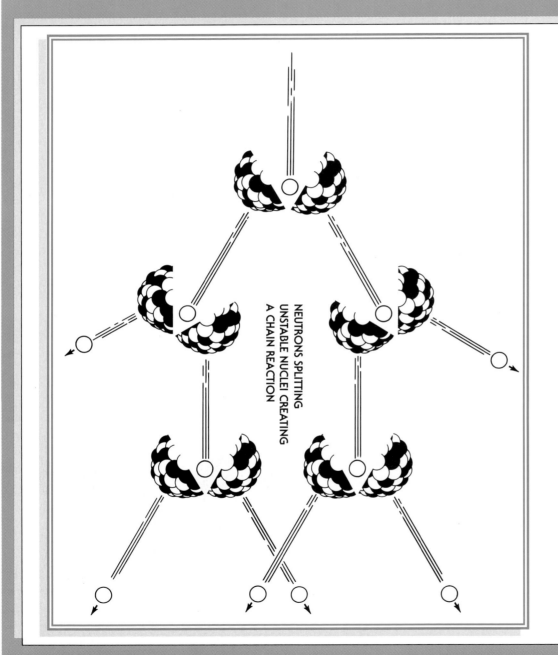

NEUTRONS SPLITTING
UNSTABLE NUCLEI CREATING
A CHAIN REACTION

completely vaporized in the first second of the explosion. Windows rattled 250 miles away, and a blinding light momentarily banished the early morning darkness. Gen. Thomas F. Farrell, who witnessed the test from a bunker five miles away, later described the spectacle:

The effects could well be called…magnificent, beautiful, stupendous, and terrifying…. The lighting effects beggared description. The whole country was lighted…with an intensity many times that of the midday sun. It was golden, purple, violet, gray, and blue…. Thirty seconds after the explosion, came, first the air blast, pressing hard against people and things,…followed almost immediately by the strong, sustained, awesome roar which warned of doomsday and made us feel that we puny things were blasphemous to dare tamper with the forces heretofore [formerly] reserved to the Almighty.

Minutes after the test, President Truman received news of its success. The United States, he realized, now had nearly unlimited power at its disposal. But should the Americans unleash such destructive power on other human beings?

The Decision to Drop the Bomb

Truman and his advisers considered several factors in deciding whether or not to use the new atomic device. A few of the president's advisers argued that using the bomb would be morally wrong. They pointed out that the weapon's blast would be so huge that there would be no way to avoid killing thousands of civilians while striking at military targets. They were also against

Harry S Truman

Raised on a Missouri farm, Harry Truman (1884–1972) earned the nickname "Give 'em hell Harry" for his courage and frankness. He served with distinction on the fields of France in World War I, fighting in several major battles. After returning home in 1919, he married Elizabeth (Bess) Wallace, his childhood sweetheart. Truman then operated a clothing store in Kansas City. After the store went out of business, he entered public service, working his way up through a number of local political offices. In 1934, he became a U.S. senator, and in 1944, he was President Roosevelt's running mate. On April 12, 1945, Roosevelt died and Truman became president. The huge responsibilities of running the mammoth war effort and leading the free world now rested on Truman's shoulders. He worked hard to carry out Roosevelt's plans for the defeat of the Axis powers. The most important decision of his life came only months later when he chose to drop atomic bombs on two Japanese cities. After the war, Truman played an important role in the creation of the United Nations and won the presidential election of 1948. Most historians remember him as one of the hardest working, most honest, and most intelligent of the country's presidents.

President Harry S Truman made the decision to drop the atom bomb on Japan.

Horror in the Sea

After being damaged by a kamikaze attack on March 31, 1945, the USS *Indianapolis* docked in San Francisco for repairs. There, it received its orders to deliver the uranium for the first atom bomb, or A-bomb, to Tinian Island in the Marianas. On July 30, only four days after completing its mission to Tinian, the *Indianapolis* suffered a fatal hit from a torpedo launched by a Japanese submarine. The ship sank so fast, there was no time to send out a call for help. For more than two

days, no one knew the ship had gone down, so no relief vessels were sent. Of the 1,200 men aboard the doomed ship, 800 survived the attack. They spent nearly 3 1/2 days in the ocean, with no food, no drinking water, and no way to sleep or even rest. The ordeal was made worse when swarms of sharks attacked, dragging hundreds of the sailors to gruesome deaths. Managing to beat the sharks back with boards and other debris, 316 of the *Indianapolis* crew survived long enough to be rescued.

The USS Indianapolis *delivered the uranium used in the first atom bomb.*

"Little Boy," the atom bomb that was dropped on Hiroshima.

Col. Paul Tibbets, the pilot of the Enola Gay, had a dangerous and important mission—to drop the atom bomb on Hiroshima.

using the bomb because it was not needed, they claimed. The ongoing blockade and bombing of Japanese cities had already nearly destroyed Japan. According to this view, it was only a matter of time before the enemy would have to surrender.

But Secretary Stimson and Truman were unmoved by these arguments. They had weighed the consequences of *not* using the bomb. U.S. strategists told the president that the invasion of Japan would take one year or more and would cost at least half a million American and several million Japanese lives. And Stimson pointed out that the Japanese would likely fight to the death. It was better, he said, to kill a few thousand with the bomb and end the war quickly than allow millions to die in an invasion. Also, he insisted, the United States should not be moved by moral considerations. After all, the Japanese had not been concerned about the morality of their sneak attack on Pearl Harbor, the savage mistreatment of American prisoners, and the brutal kamikaze attacks. Truman agreed and later wrote, "I regarded the bomb as a weapon and never had any doubt that it should be used." Winston Churchill sent word that he favored the bomb's use if it could bring an early end to the war.

Having determined that they would drop the bomb, the American leaders now had to choose the targets. Some said Kyoto, the ancient capital, should be destroyed first. But Stimson disagreed, pointing out that the city housed Japan's greatest cultural and religious shrines and, therefore, should be spared. Truman agreed, writing in his private journal, "Even if the Japs are savages, ruthless, merciless and fanatic, we as the leader of the free world for the common welfare cannot drop this terrible bomb on the old capital or the new [Tokyo]." The targets finally agreed upon were Hiroshima, Kikura, Niigata, and Nagasaki, all centers of industry and war production.

The first atom bomb destroyed much of Hiroshima. A crew member on board the Enola Gay took this photograph minutes after the bomb was dropped.

Flight of the Enola Gay

The final series of events leading to the dropping of the atomic bomb went like clockwork. On July 24, 1945, the U.S. cruiser *Indianapolis* delivered lead buckets containing the uranium needed for the bomb to Tinian Island in the Marianas. The captain of the ship was unaware of the contents of the buckets. His orders were that if his ship sank, he should save the containers at all costs, putting them in lifeboats if necessary. That same day, planes from the United States arrived with other essential bomb parts. Scientists on Tinian assembled the first bomb, nicknamed Little Boy, during the next few days. They did not arm it, fearing that if the plane carrying it crashed during takeoff, the entire island would be blown up. They decided instead to arm the weapon in the air shortly before reaching the target.

On July 26, 1945, the United States and the Allies issued a final ultimatum to Japan, demanding unconditional surrender. The message concluded, "The alternative for Japan is prompt and utter destruction." When the Japanese refused, Truman grimly commented that there is "no alternative now."

On August 5, 1945, technicians on Tinian loaded the world's first nuclear weapon onto a B-29 called *Enola Gay*. The pilot, Col. Paul Tibbets, had named the plane after his mother. Two other B-29s, carrying military observers and cameras, would accompany the *Enola Gay*.

The planes glided off the Tinian runway at 2:45 A.M. on August 6. They reached the initial target, Hiroshima, a city of 340,000, at about 8:05 A.M. At exactly 8:15, the *Enola Gay's* bombardier discharged the four-ton Little Boy, and the plane lurched

The Destruction of Hiroshima and Nagasaki

The world entered the nuclear age at a great cost in human lives and suffering. The earlier conventional firebombing of Tokyo killed more people and destroyed more buildings than either of the A-bombs dropped on Hiroshima (August 6, 1945) and Nagasaki (August 9, 1945). Yet the realization that such devastation could come in an instant from a single bomb was terrifying. In Hiroshima, the blast completely leveled more than four of the six square miles that made up the city. The searing heat melted steel girders like candle wax. People standing near the center of the blast were totally vaporized, leaving only their shadows burned into nearby concrete walls. Thousands were torn to shreds by flying clouds of glass, wood, and other debris or were buried alive by collapsing buildings.

The destruction on Hiroshima and Nagasaki was severe and immediate. Few buildings remained standing.

Radiation from the atom bombs killed or maimed thousands of Japanese. Here, a man and girl tend to a boy's legs, burned by radiation.

Many who survived the initial blasts suffered from severe radiation sickness within two weeks. They vomited uncontrollably, spit up blood, and died in agony. Some people on the outskirts of the city looked directly at the fireball and went blind. In the following years, thousands more died of leukemia and other cancers caused by the radiation. Medical authorities estimate that the death toll from all these causes for the two cities exceeded 300,000. Secretary of War Henry Stimson was moved to say, "Now, with the release of atomic energy, man's ability to destroy himself is very nearly complete. The bombs… ended a war. They also made it wholly clear that we must never have another war. This is the lesson… [people] everywhere must learn… There is no other choice."

upward in response to the sudden loss of weight. Tibbets then banked the plane away at a steep angle in order to avoid the effects of the coming blast. A few seconds later, the bomb automatically detonated, or exploded, at an altitude of eighteen hundred feet. An arc of blinding light seemed to tear the sky apart.

"My God!" murmured a startled crew member. Another said, "Suddenly a glaring whitish pink light appeared in the sky accompanied by an unnatural tremor that was followed almost immediately by a wave of suffocating heat and wind that swept everything away in its path." As a gigantic mushroom cloud rose into the atmosphere, Tibbets swung the plane around for a better view. "It was like looking over a tar barrel boiling," he said. "We couldn't see the city at all through the thin layer of dust." In fact, there was little left to see. Most of Hiroshima had simply ceased to exist.

A Rain of Ruin

The reactions to the bombing of Hiroshima were immediate and emotional. The shocked Japanese called the destruction "barbaric." Radio Tokyo reported: "The impact of the bomb is so terrific that practically all living things, human and animals, literally were seared to death by the tremendous heat and pressure engendered by the blast. All the dead and injured were burned beyond recognition." Early estimates suggested that more than seventy thousand people died in the initial blast alone. More perished each hour from serious injuries or in the fires that raged through the ruins. The Japanese leaders charged, "This diabolical weapon brands the United States for ages to come as a destroyer of justice and of mankind."

Truman announced the official U.S. position on August 7, saying, "The force from which the sun draws its power has been loosed upon those who brought war to the Far East." The president warned, "If they [the Japanese] do not now accept our terms, they may expect a rain of ruin from the air, the like of which has never been seen on this earth."

When the Japanese still did not surrender, a group of B-29s dropped a second atomic bomb two days later, on August 9. This time, the target was Nagasaki, a city of 250,000 located on the island of Kyushu. The nearly total destruction of the city sent a wave of fear through the country. Japanese leaders met that night to debate surrender. The most extreme militarists argued that the country should fight on. They insisted that every Japanese citizen should die rather than surrender. Those who felt that surrender was better than annihilation called upon Emperor Hirohito to decide. For years, the Japanese people had fought a bloody war for the honor of their "living god." Now, as they teetered on the brink of total destruction, their fate was in his hands.

CHAPTER SEVEN

"A Better World Shall Emerge"— Surrender and Aftermath

On the night of August 9, 1945, when the most powerful of Japan's leaders met to discuss the Allied surrender terms, no one in the room doubted that the outlook for the nation was grim. All over the empire, Japanese armies had been crushed and defeated. The Imperial Navy was gone. The United States had Japan surrounded and blockaded and had demolished more than one hundred cities with conventional bombs. And only hours before, the second of the new superbombs had obliterated Nagasaki. The United States now threatened to use more A-bombs and blast Japan back into the Stone Age.

The Decision to Surrender

With the Japanese leadership evenly divided between those who wanted to continue fighting and those who thought surrender was the only sane option, the emperor broke the deadlock. He expressed his desire that the surrender be accepted on one condition—that the status of the emperor be preserved, that the "living god" be allowed to continue as a figurehead for the Japanese people. This proposal was sent to the Allies the next day.

The Americans, too, were divided about surrender terms. Hearing the Japanese condition, many U.S. leaders angrily advised the president to reject the proposal. One congressman said, "Let the Japs know…what unconditional surrender means. Let the dirty rats squeal." But others were more willing to compromise. Secretary Stimson, with his usual voice of reason, pointed out that the emperor was perhaps the only person who could

These Japanese soldiers, confined to a prisoner-of-war camp in Guam, appear sullen after hearing the news of Japan's surrender. Japanese citizens reacted to the news with disbelief, grief, and shame.

order the Japanese armies all over Southeast Asia to surrender peacefully. Agreeing to the emperor's condition was the only way of saving "us from a score of bloody Iwo Jimas and Okinawas," Stimson said.

The Americans compromised. They sent word to the Japanese that the surrender would have to remain unconditional. The status of the emperor would be decided by the supreme commander of the Allied forces and by a public ballot of the Japanese people. Essentially, this meant that if all went well, the emperor would be retained.

The Japanese war hawks were upset by the Allied reply. Arguments dragged on for four more days. Finally, the emperor told the militarists, "Bow to my wishes and accept the Allied reply." Hours later, on August 15, 1945, Hirohito issued a radio broadcast to the Japanese people, almost none of whom had ever heard his voice before. He called for an end to the "bloodshed and cruelty" and added, "Should we continue to fight, it would not only result in the ultimate collapse of the Japanese nation, but also . . . the total extinction of human civilization." He conceded that surrender was an unbearable choice. "Nevertheless," he said sadly, "the time has come when we must bear the

The War's Grim Toll

The Pacific War caused death and destruction on a vast scale. The human loss was staggering. Nearly 17 million people died. More than 13 million of those were Chinese, slaughtered during the brutal Japanese invasions. More than 50,000 Americans died as well as 40,000 British, 30,000 Australians, and 10,000 New Zealanders. A total of more than 1.7 million Japanese soldiers and civilians were killed, and more than 120 Japanese cities were totally or partially destroyed. The wounded of all nationalities numbered well over 20 million. At least 10 million children became orphans.

The war's materiel losses were also huge. The United States lost twenty-three large warships, including five aircraft carriers. Sixty-six large Japanese warships sank, as well as dozens of submarines and more than twenty-three hundred cargo and supply vessels. Each side lost thousands of planes.

The war somehow touched every country, every community, every family. Journalist Eric Sevareid said of the conflict, "The shock waves it sent through our societies, our institutions and our nervous systems have not yet died away."

Allied and Japanese forces suffered heavy losses during the war in the Pacific. Ceremonial boxes containing the ashes of some of Hiroshima's cremated victims are stacked behind this mourning Japanese man.

More than 50,000 Americans died during the war in the Pacific. These servicemen ponder the true cost of war.

For Some, the War Never Ended

Marooned on tiny and remote Pacific islands, some Japanese soldiers did not know when the war ended. Rescuers found many of them in the years following the Japanese surrender. A few soldiers, however, either never found out or refused to believe that the conflict was over. In 1951, nineteen Japanese soldiers on one of the Mariana Islands finally surrendered. Hiru Onada and Kinishi Kozuka held out on a small Philippine island for decades because their commander had ordered them never to surrender. After being discovered in 1972, they exchanged gunfire with Philippine police and Kozuka was killed. Onada then hid in the forest. In 1974, his former commander flew to the island and persuaded him to give up. Former private Teruo Nakamura discovered the war was over in 1975 after hiding out on an island in Indonesia for thirty-three years. During all that time, he believed in his heart that Japan had won the war and that his people would eventually come to take him home. Some Japanese authorities believe that other Japanese troops continue to maintain the honor of the empire in forgotten corners of the wide Pacific.

The Guns Silent at Last

In the two weeks following the emperor's fateful broadcast, a huge array of American and British warships converged on Japan. Hundreds of landing craft and transport planes poured more than twenty thousand occupation troops into the home islands. Into Tokyo Bay cruised the forty-five-thousand-ton USS *Missouri*, flagship of the U.S. Pacific fleet, followed by dozens of Allied support ships. The formal surrender came on Sunday morning, September 2, 1945, three years, eight months, and twenty-five days after Japanese planes attacked Pearl Harbor. A nine-member Japanese delegation, led by Foreign Minister Mamoru Shigemitsu, boarded the *Missouri*, where hundreds of U.S. and Allied officers and soldiers waited. The Japanese were tense, obviously gripped by emotion, yet highly dignified. They walked to the table on which rested the surrender documents. Then, Gen. Douglas MacArthur, representing the Allied forces, approached a microphone and said:

unbearable." The Japanese people reacted first with disbelief, then with grief and shame. But nearly all did their best to support the decision of their emperor.

Allied planes fly in formation over Allied vessels near the Japanese coast. The planes then flew over Tokyo in one final show of strength.

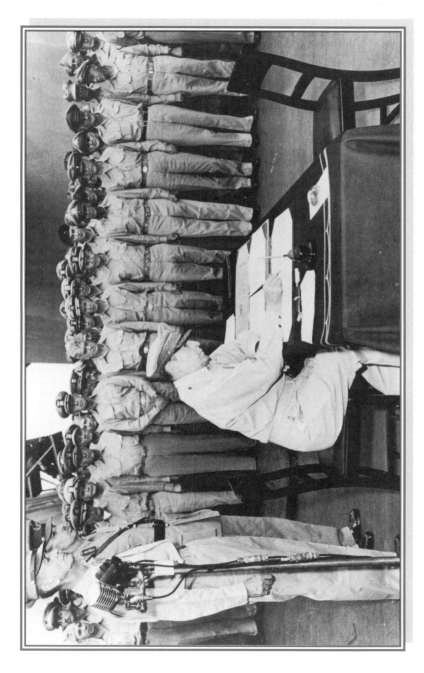

Seated at a desk on board the USS Missouri, Gen. Douglas MacArthur signs Japan's surrender documents and officially ends the war in the Pacific.

We are gathered here, representatives of the major warring powers, to conclude a solemn agreement whereby peace may be restored.... It is my earnest hope and indeed the hope of all mankind that from this ... occasion a better world shall emerge out of the blood and carnage of the past—a world founded upon faith and understanding—a world dedicated to the dignity of man and the fulfillment of his most cherished wish—for freedom, tolerance and justice.

When MacArthur finished speaking, the Japanese sat at the table and signed the documents. Then, MacArthur signed, along with other Allied leaders, including Adm. Chester Nimitz and representatives of China, Great Britain, Australia, and the Soviet Union. Finally, General MacArthur spoke again: "Let us pray for peace ...and that God will preserve it always. These proceedings are closed." Seconds later, a gigantic flight of two thousand Allied planes passed over the ship, and then over Tokyo, in a final majestic demonstration of power. In the words of the historian Louis L. Snyder, "Thus, came to an end the long, tragic trail from Bataan and Corregidor through New Guinea, the Marianas, and the Philippines to Japan. The guns at last were silent."

Americans in New York (below) and other U.S. cities were jubilant when they learned the Japanese bad surrendered.

Japan Rises from the Ashes

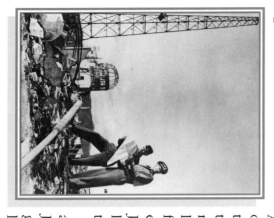

With MacArthur acting as supreme Allied commander, the United States began the tremendous task of rebuilding Japan and making it an ally rather than a foe of the free world. This was the official policy of the Allies and was carried out in Germany and Italy as well. In Japan, Emperor Hirohito joined in the effort, instructing his people to "win the confidence of the world" by obeying Japan's commitments to the surrender terms.

One of the first orders of business was to eliminate the aggressive elements of Japanese society that might cause trouble in the future. MacArthur ordered the new Japanese leaders to remove more than 200,000 militaristic politicians, army officers, and local leaders from their posts. Twenty-five of Japan's top-ranking leaders were tried as war criminals for giving the orders in Japan's war of aggression. Seven, including the infamous Hideki Tojo, received death sentences and died by hanging on December 23, 1948. The other eighteen "minor" war criminals were convicted of crimes such as the murder and mistreatment of prisoners of war. About one thousand received death sentences.

In 1947, MacArthur introduced a new constitution for Japan. It set up independent courts and judges, gave guarantees of political freedoms, provided voting rights for all adults, and allowed women to own property for the first time in Japan's history. Most Japanese were pleased by these changes. Article Nine of the new constitution was especially important. It stated that Japan forever renounced "war as a sovereign right of the nation and the threat or use of force as a means of settling international disputes." In effect, the Allies stripped Japan of its military strength and allowed it to maintain only a small local defense force.

Other far-reaching new measures transformed Japan. The Americans restructured Japanese industry, allowing production only of non-war-related commodities. The entire educational system underwent reform. The new system de-emphasized the teaching of traditional, aggressive ideals and stressed Western methods and courses of study. In addition, there were sweeping land reforms. For centuries, most of the land was owned by a few wealthy individuals. Poor peasants worked the land in exchange for some of the food grown. MacArthur decreed that Japan's millions of peasant farmers could now own their own land. By 1950, 90 percent of the country's farms had become thriving independent businesses.

In order to aid in economic reconstruction, thousands of U.S. advisers and business experts traveled to Japan. They taught the Japanese how to set up Western-style businesses and trade their goods on the world market. At the same time, billions of U.S. dollars poured into Japan to help support the rebirth of the nation.

By the time the official Pacific War Treaty went into effect in 1952, Japan had become an ally and trading partner of its former enemies. This remarkable transformation was made possible in part by the practical, farsighted attitudes of Allied leaders. They believed it was more constructive for all nations concerned if the war's winners helped the losers recover. They reasoned that punishing the losers would only hinder economic growth on both sides as well as perpetuate hatred and sow the seeds for future unrest.

In 1952, Japan's premier, Shigeru Yoshida, thanked the Allies for creating "a magnanimous [generous] peace unparalleled in history." He added, "The Japan of today is no longer the Japan of yesterday. We will not fail your expectations of us as a new nation, dedicated to peace, democracy and freedom."

A New World Order Takes Shape

The events of the war in the Pacific helped to dramatically alter the balance of power among nations. First, the United States, because of its giant industrial complex and its sole possession of the atom bomb, became, for all practical purposes, invincible. In fact, the United States entered the postwar era as the most powerful nation in history. Significantly, for the first time in memory, a nation with overwhelming strength did not use it to suppress or conquer others. Instead, the United States sought to use its might to maintain peace and help its former enemies.

But the reign as the world's only superpower did not last long. The Soviet Union soon showed that it too was a great power to be reckoned with. The Soviet leadership had been shrewd. All through the war, the Soviets had concentrated on fighting the Germans and had stayed out of the Pacific War. When the United States finally defeated Japan, the Soviets became worried. They sensed that they would be left out of important postwar agreements in the Pacific. So, at midnight on August 8, 1945, just days before the Japanese surrender, the Soviet Union declared war on Japan. This automatically made the Soviet Union one of the victors in the war. Since the victors shared in shaping the future politics of the region, the Soviets were now assured a voice in that process.

An even more important development happened in the late 1940s, when the Soviets developed their own atomic bomb. There were now two superpowers in the world. What followed was nearly four decades of cold war—tension and mistrust between the two nations. Each sought to intimidate the other by building more and better nuclear weapons. The device that had been conceived to end World War II became, in peacetime, an object of fear that threatened to engulf the world in nuclear destruction.

Modern Japan— Economic Leader

The modern Japanese are as aggressive and industrious as their World War II predecessors. But today, it is the business world and not other nations they seek to conquer. During the Allied occupation and miraculous rebuilding of postwar Japan, the Japanese people learned to channel their energies into the production of useful goods for trade on the world market.

By the 1960s, Japanese technology, research, and manufacturing methods had caught up with and surpassed those of most other countries. Well-built Japanese cars flooded the U.S. market in the 1970s and 1980s, outselling many American models. Japanese-made electronic products such as stereos, TVs, and compact-disc players now dominate the world electronics market.

Japanese businesspeople also learned to invest wisely the huge profits they made from world trade. In the 1980s, Japanese firms bought several giant U.S. companies, office buildings, and other real estate. Some Americans see this as a threat to the U.S. economy. Others predict that economic competition will be healthy for both countries. "No matter what happens," quipped one American businessman, "it sure beats shooting at each other."

A Future Without War?

A more positive development of the post-World War II era was the formation of the United Nations (UN) in 1945. Representatives from fifty-one nations met in San Francisco and drew up an initial charter. The main objective of the organization was to bring lasting peace to the world. The UN charter opens with the historic line: "We the Peoples of the United Nations [are] determined to save succeeding generations from the scourge of war, which twice in our lifetime has brought untold sorrow to mankind."

Other aims of the UN are to uphold fundamental human rights, to maintain international law, and to promote social progress and better living standards. By 1989, membership in the UN had grown to 159 countries. The organization continues to work for the improvement of international relations, striving to fulfill the hope voiced by MacArthur that "a better world shall emerge out of the blood and carnage of the past."

This was the same hope expressed by Winston Churchill in the darkest days of the great global conflict. "We now have a chance," he said, "of avoiding the errors of previous generations.... People cry out for peace and joy.... Before us lies the realization of the dream of the poor—that they shall live in peace, protected by our invincible power from aggression and evil."

Unfortunately, this hope of MacArthur, Churchill, and others who lived through the agony of World War II remains largely unfulfilled. There have been many other armed conflicts in the world since 1945, including wars in Korea, Vietnam, and the Persian Gulf, as well as numerous rebellions and incidents of civil strife. There are those who say this proves war is inevitable.

Yet others say this belief that there will always be war assumes that humanity will never progress. They have hope that people will someday learn to refrain from using war to solve disputes. Many believe that given enough time, the United Nations will become increasingly effective in achieving its primary goal—to prevent war. As Louis L. Snyder put it, "For those who believe in human progress there is the hope that, despite the fears and insecurity of the present, there may be a better future."

Allies the countries aligned against Japan, Germany, and Italy during World War II.

artillery large ground-based guns.

Axis the alliance of Japan, Germany, and Italy during World War II.

Banzai in Japanese, "May you live a thousand years!"; screamed by Japanese soldiers in suicidal charges against the Allies.

battleship a large, heavily armored warship with many large guns.

beachhead a captured section of enemy shoreline.

Bushido code set of rules imposed by the Japanese on conquered peoples, threatening to kill anyone who harmed a Japanese person.

camouflage ways of concealing oneself by blending in with natural surroundings.

commandos fighters specially trained for dangerous missions.

convoy a group of ships or vehicles traveling together and usually protected by armed guards.

cruiser a small, fast warship with limited firepower.

cryptologist an expert at making and breaking complicated codes.

destroyer a medium-size warship armed with guns and torpedoes.

expansionist a person or nation that seeks to increase its territory, power, and influence.

feudal society one in which a powerful lord allows people to work the land in return for military service.

fire storm a powerful wind created by drafts of heated air during a massive fire.

fission the process by which atoms split and release large amounts of energy, as in an atomic bomb.

flagship a vessel that carries the commander of a fleet and serves as the headquarters for the fleet.

garrison a military post or the troops stationed in it.

hara-kiri, or seppuku a form of ritual suicide practiced in Japan consisting of tearing through the stomach and chest with a knife or sword.

incendiary an explosive designed to create fires.

isolationist a person or nation that seeks to avoid getting involved in the problems of other countries.

kamikazes Japanese pilots in World War II who committed suicide by crashing their planes into Allied ships.

samurai the traditional Japanese warrior class.

Seabees American engineers who specialize in building roads, bridges, and airfields in captured territories.

shogun a supreme feudal lord in ancient Japan.

squadron a group of ten to twenty or more planes or a section of a naval fleet.

task force a group of ships or other military units gathered to carry out specific orders.

USO United Services Organization; a group of performers formed during World War II to entertain American troops.

USS abbreviation for United States Ship.

For Further Reading

Bruce Blevin, Jr., *From Pearl Harbor to Okinawa, The War in the Pacific: 1941–1945.* New York: Random House, 1960.

Jane Claypool, *Hiroshima and Nagasaki.* New York: Franklin Watts, 1984.

Robert Leckie, *Great American Battles.* New York: Random House, 1968.

Ronald Lewin, *The American Magic: Codes, Ciphers, and the Defeat of Japan.* New York: Farrar, Straus & Giroux, 1982.

Walter Lord, *Day of Infamy.* New York: Henry Holt, 1957.

Roger Manvell, *Films of the Second World War.* New York: Dell, 1974.

Reader's Digest Association, ed., *The World at Arms: The Reader's Digest Illustrated History of World War II.* London: Reader's Digest Association, 1989.

Clark G. Reynolds, *The Fast Carriers: The Forging of an Air Navy.* New York: McGraw-Hill, 1968.

Robert L. Reynolds, *Commodore Perry in Japan.* New York: American Heritage, 1963.

Louis L. Snyder, *World War II.* New York: Franklin Watts, 1981.

Works Consulted

Winston Churchill, *The Second World War*. New York: Bantam Books, 1962.

John Costello, *The Pacific War*. New York: Rawson, Wade, 1981.

Hans Dollinger, *The Decline and Fall of Nazi Germany and Japan*. New York: Bonanza Books, 1968.

Jack Levien and John Lord, *Winston Churchill: The Valiant Years*. New York: Scholastic Book Services, 1962.

Walter Lord, *Incredible Victory*. New York: Harper & Row, 1967.

Marlene J. Mayo, ed., *The Emergence of Imperial Japan*. Lexington, MA: D.C. Heath, 1970.

Richard F. Newcomb, *Iwo Jima*. New York: Holt, Rinehart & Winston, 1965.

Gordon W. Prange, *At Dawn We Slept: The Untold Story of Pearl Harbor*. New York: McGraw-Hill, 1981.

Edwin O. Reischauer, *Japan: The Story of a Nation*. New York: Alfred A. Knopf, 1970.

Martin J. Sherwin, *A World Destroyed: The Atomic Bomb and the Grand Alliance*. New York: Vintage Books, 1977.

Louis L. Snyder, *The War: A Concise History, 1939–1945*. New York: Dell, 1960.

Ronald H. Spector, *Eagle Against the Sun, The American War with Japan*. New York: The Free Press, 1985.

John Toland, *The Rising Sun: The Decline and Fall of the Japanese Empire, 1936–1945*. New York: Random House, 1970.

Richard Tregaskis, *Guadalcanal Diary*. New York: Random House, 1943.

aircraft carriers, 59
Akagi, 47, 49
Aleutian Islands, 44
Amaterasu, 10, 11
Anti-Comintern Pact, 15
atomic bomb
  debate over, 77, 79
  German efforts to develop, 74
  researching of, 73, 74
  targets of, 79
  testing of, 75, 77
Australia, 30, 41, 87
  Japanese threat to, 50
  fighting on New Guinea, 56
  Guadalcanal battle ended, 57
Axis alliance, 31
  formation of, 16
  industrial production compared to U.S., 53

Bataan, 37, 64
  death march, 37, 39, 58
  movie about, 45
  surrender at, 39
Batavia, 41
Battle of Leyte Gulf, 64-65
Battle of Midway, 22
  established role of naval air power, 50
  Japanese strategy, 42, 44, 48
  losses from, 50
battleships, 32, 33, 46, 47, 50, 68
Bohr, Niels, 73, 74
Burma, 34, 41
Bushido, code of, 35

Canada
  declaration of war against Japan, 30
cancer, 81
Capra, Frank, 45
Caroline island chains, 60, 62
Chamberlain, William, 28
China, 34, 87
  Japanese invasion of
    death toll, 85
    propaganda films about, 45
  Japanese threats toward, 15
Churchill, Winston, 30, 90
  reaction to U.S. joining war, 31
  remarks after Roosevelt's death, 71
  support for atomic bomb, 74, 79
cold war, 89
Corregidor, 39, 64, 65

Doolittle, James, 38, 41, 42, 45

Einstein, Albert, 73
  letter to Roosevelt, 74
Enola Gay, 79, 80

Farrell, Thomas E., 77

Fermi, Enrico, 74
feudalism, 13-14
Flannigan, G.S., 24
Ford, John, 45
France, 31
Fuchida, Mitsuo, 22, 25

Genda, Minoru, 22
Germany, 31, 88
  atomic bomb research, 74
  invasion of Poland, 19
Gilbert Islands, 60, 62
Great Britain, 22, 59, 87
  declaration of war against Japan, 30-31
  Japanese attacks on colonies of, 29, 32
  U.S. aid to, 55
Great Depression, 15, 17
Greater East Asia Prosperity Sphere, 20
Groves, Leslie R., 75
Guadalcanal, 45
  Allied capture of, 60
  U.S. attack on, 55, 57
Guam, 29, 32, 84

hara-kiri, 13, 18
  American attitude toward, 58, 61
  on Saipan Island, 61
Hawaii. *See* Midway Island; Pearl Harbor
Hirohito, Emperor, 10, 42
  decision to surrender, 82, 83, 84
  announcement of, 84, 86
  role during reconstruction, 88
Hiroshima, dropping of atomic bomb on, 80
  damage reports, 81, 82
  eyewitness accounts, 82
Hitler, Adolf, 15, 16, 19, 32
Holmes, Jasper, 44
Hong Kong, 29, 32

Indochina, 20, 32
isolationism, 16, 19, 30
Italy, 31, 88
Iwo Jima, 46, 66, 73
  casualties, 67
  eyewitness account of, 68

Japan
  civilian population
    growth of, 15
    propaganda's effect on, 61
    war's effect on, 66
  colonial policies of, 35
  emperor's role in, 10, 11, 14
  expansionism of, 9, 14, 15, 19-20
    early in the war, 32, 42
    U.S. fight against, 55, 57, 60
  feudal era, 13
  government of
    anti-foreign attitude, 9, 20, 40
    propaganda, 8, 45, 58
  military of, 65
    air force, 23, 34
    army, 33-34
      compared to U.S., 59
    refusal to surrender, 66, 72, 80, 86
    samurai tradition, 12, 15, 34
    Western efforts to limit, 15
    worship of death, 58
  modernization period of, 14
    need for raw materials, 41
  postwar
    constitution, 88
    economy, 90
    reconstruction, 36, 88
    propaganda films, 45
  reasons for wanting war
    culture, 7
    national survival, 8
  surrender of, 86, 87
    U.S. policy toward
    blockade of (1945), 65
    bombing of, 65, 70
    occupation of, 86, 88
  Western influence in, 13, 14

Japanese-Americans
  in U.S. Army, 51
  internment in concentration camps, 50, 51

Java, 34, 41
jungle fighting, 56

kamikazes, 68, 69
  damage inflicted by, 71, 78
Kellogg-Briand Pact, 19
Kenney, George C., 66
Kenworth, Jesse, 25
Kimmel, Husband E., 25
Korean War, 36
Kozuka, Kinishi, 86

Latin America, 31
Leyte Gulf, Battle of, 64-65
Lindbergh, Charles, 30
"Little Boy," 79, 80

MacArthur, Douglas, 60
  at Japan's surrender, 86, 87
  career of, 36
  during Japanese reconstruction, 88
  in the Philippines, 35, 37, 63, 65
McCallum, Charles, 56
McClusky, Wade, 48
Malaya, 32, 34
Manchester, William, 68
Manchuria, 15
Manhattan Project, 73, 74, 75
  see also atomic bomb

Mariana Islands, 60
  battle on Saipan Island, 61
    casualties, 61
  Japanese who would not surrender, 86
Marshall Islands, 46, 60, 62
Midway Island battle of, 41
  Japanese strategy, 42, 44
    miscalculations in, 44, 48
  U.S. cracking of secret code, 43
militarism, 11, 13
Morison, Samuel, 46, 57, 65
movies, 45

Nagasaki, 82
Nagumo, Chuichi, 20, 22
  at Midway, 47-48
  death of, 61
Nakamura, Teruo, 86
nationalism, 14
Nazis, 15, 19
New Guinea
  Australian recapture of, 60
  battle on, 56
New Zealand, 50
Nimitz, Chester W., 44, 59
  at Japanese surrender, 87
  impact on naval strategy, 46, 47, 50
nuclear fission, 74, 76

Okinawa, 66, 73
  sinking of the *Yamato*, 68
Oldendorf, Jesse B., 64
Onada, Hiru, 86
Operation Coronet, 73
Operation Mi, 42
Operation Olympic, 73
Oppenheimer, J. Robert, 75

Pacific War Treaty, 89
Pearl Harbor, 7, 8
  Japanese attack on, 29
    deaths from, 24, 25
    effect on U.S. Navy, 29, 31
    planning of, 22
    public reaction to, 29
    reasons for, 20
    revisionist view of, 28
Perry, Matthew, 13
Philippine Islands, 34
  Japanese conquest of, 39, 41
    at Bataan, 37, 39
    reasons for, 34-35, 63
  U.S. reconquest of
    assault on Leyte Island, 63-65
Phillips, Tom, 33
Poland, 19
Prince of Wales, 32, 33, 34, 50
prisoners of war, 41, 61
  Japan's cruelty toward, 56, 58, 88
  on Bataan death march, 37, 39
propaganda
  in movies, 45

Japanese, 8, 58, 61
racism
  Japanese, 9, 11, 14, 15, 20
  U.S., 50, 51
radiation sickness, 81
religion, 7
Repulse, 32, 33, 34, 50
Rockwell, Norman, 54
Romulo, Carlos, 63
Roosevelt, Franklin D., 17
  death of, 71-72, 77
  Manhattan Project, 74
  response to Pearl Harbor, 28, 29
Rosenthal, Joe, 67
Rosie the Riveter, 54
Russell Islands, 60
Russo-Japanese War (1904-1905), 14
Rutherford, Ernest, 73

Saipan Island, 61
samurai code, 34
  influence of, 12, 15
  ritual suicide, 13, 69. *See* hara-kiri
seppuku. *See* hara-kiri
Seabees, 59, 60
secret codes, 43, 44
Sevareid, Eric, 85
shoguns, 10, 12, 13
Singapore, 29, 32
Sino-Japanese War (1894-1895), 14
Snyder, Louis L., 55, 87, 90
Solomon Islands, 46, 60
Soviet Union, 87
  postwar power of, 89
  U.S. aid to, 55
Sprague, C.A.F., 65
Stimson, Henry L., 75, 81
  arguments for using bomb, 79
  Japanese surrender proposal, 83-84

Talen, Maria, 67
Tasaka, Tomotaka, 45
Thailand, 32
Tibbets, Paul, 79, 80, 82
Tojo, Hideki, 18
  ascendancy to war minister, 19-20
  attack on Pearl Harbor, 22, 31
  death sentence, 88
Tokyo
  firestorm, 65, 70, 81
  first American raid on, 38, 41, 42
  trade, 13, 14, 34, 88, 90
Truman, Harry S, 36, 72
  decision to use atomic bomb, 77, 79
Tyler, Kermit, 22, 27

United Nations, 77, 90
United States
  Congress
    declaration of war, 29
    efforts during the war, 53
    laws opposing war, 19

domestic efforts for the war, 50
internment of Japanese-Americans, 50, 51
  propaganda films, 45
  rationing, 50, 52
foreign policy
  1854 opening of Japan, 13-14
  isolationist tradition, 16, 19
  postwar influence, 89
government system, 9
industrial production, 31, 53
  after the war, 89
  growth of, 59
  women's impact on, 54, 55
military
  growth of in Pacific, 59
Japanese-Americans in, 51
  war strategy, 57, 72
  women in, 54

USS *Arizona*, 21
  sinking of, 24, 25
USS *California*, 21, 25
USS *Colorado*, 21
USS *Enterprise*, 21, 31
  at Battle of Midway, 48, 49
  kamikaze attack on, 71
USS *Hornet*, 38, 49
USS *Indianapolis*, 78
USS *Lexington*, 21, 31
USS *Maryland*, 8, 21, 25
USS *Missouri*, 86, 87
USS *Oklahoma*, 8, 21, 25
USS *Solace*, 71
USS *Tennessee*, 24, 25
USS *West Virginia*, 21, 25
USS *Yorktown*, 49, 50

Wake Island, 29, 32
war, 7, 8, 9
war trials, 88
Wheeler, Burton K., 29
women, 53, 54
World War I, 16, 19
World War II (Pacific)
  bombing raids, 38, 41, 42, 65, 70
    atomic, 80-82
  chronology of, 6
  death toll, 85
  declaration of, 29, 30-31
  ending of, 82-84, 86, 89
  industry's role in, 53-55
  Japan's early successes, 32, 41, 42
  secret codes during, 43, 44
  turning points of, 42, 50, 55

Yamamoto, Isoroku, 40, 49
  strategy for Midway, 41, 42
Yoshida, Shigeru, 89

Zero, 23

Photo Credits

Cover photo by FPG International

Mary Ahrndt, 43 (right)

AIP Niels Bohr Library, 74 (right)

The Bettmann Archive, 12

Harry S Truman Library, 77

Library of Congress, 27

Los Alamos National Laboratory, 74 (left), 75 (top), 79 (top)

Los Alamos Scientific Laboratory Graphic Arts Group, 75 (middle)

National Archives, 8, 10, 16, 17, 18, 22, 23, 24, 26 (all), 28, 30, 33, 34, 35, 36, 37, 38, 40, 43 (left), 46, 47 (all), 48 (both), 49, 50 (both), 51 (both), 52 (all), 53, 54 (both), 55 (both), 56 (both), 57, 59 (both), 60 (both), 61 (both), 62 (all), 63 (both), 64 (both), 66 (top), 67, 68 (all), 69, 71, 75 (bottom), 78, 84, 85 (top), 86, 87 (bottom)

National Library of Medicine, 81 (top)

Smithsonian Institution, 11, 66 (bottom), 70, 79 (bottom), 80, 81 (bottom), 85 (bottom), 87 (top), 88

About the Author

Don Nardo is an award-winning writer. He has also worked before or behind the camera in twenty films. Several of his musical compositions, including a young person's version of *The War of the Worlds* and the oratorio *Richard III*, have been played by regional orchestras. Mr. Nardo's writing credits include short stories, articles, and more than twenty books, including *Lasers: Humanity's Magic Light; Anxiety and Phobias; The Irish Potato Famine; Exercise; Gravity: The Universal Force;* and *The Mexican-American War.* Among his other writings are an episode of ABC's "Spenser: For Hire" and numerous screenplays. Mr. Nardo lives with his wife, Christine, on Cape Cod, Massachusetts.